LUCKY

LUCKY FORTUNE

Four Basic Principles to
Make Fortune Roll Your Way

Toshu Fukami

Thorsons

Thorsons
An Imprint of HarperCollins*Publishers*
77–85 Fulham Palace Road
Hammersmith, London W6 8JB
The Thorsons website address is
www.thorsons.com

First published 1997 by Tachibana Suppan Inc., Japan
This edition published by Thorsons 2000
1 3 5 7 9 10 8 6 4 2

A catalogue record of this book is
available from the British Library

ISBN 0 7225 3998 3

Printed and bound in Great Britain by
Martins the Printers Ltd, Berwick upon Tweed

CONTENTS

Preface vii

 First Basic Principle

Good Fortune Comes to Those Who Ask for It 1

Second Basic Principle

Another You Who Can Produce Either
Good Fortune or Poor Fortune 57

 Third Basic Principle

Believe in These Words
and Your Good Fortune Will Blossom 87

Fourth Basic Principle

The True Meaning of 'Praying to the Stars' 171

Logo Marks for Correctly Appealing to the Gods 237
'Divine World Good Fortune Logo' Power Marks 243

World Mate 261

PREFACE

Look around and you will see two kinds of people: 'lucky people' – for whom things almost always turn out well – and 'unlucky people' – who seem destined to fail at no matter what they attempt.

Why should it be that there are these two radically different types, since (after all) together we form the same human race? It is a question that we have all probably asked ourselves at one time or another and, as this book will show, a large part of the answer lies with the influence the spirit world has over our lives.

Nor do we tend to be content with the amount of good fortune we may be blessed with. Habitual 'losers' inevitably find themselves wishing they had a fairer amount of luck, while even people who enjoy a disproportionate amount of good fortune still tend to hope for that little bit more.

The question therefore becomes more a case of 'How can I improve my luck?'

Seeing as I am neither a psychologist nor have any medical background that would qualify me as a psychiatrist, I cannot take the psychological approach to this question of 'luck'.

However, ever since I was young I have been endowed with a more-than-average share of 'spiritual power', which I have continued to refine throughout the course of my life. Over the years I have developed my abilities to such an extent that I can see, and even commit to paper, the images of guardian spirits, or tell a person who he or she was in their past lives. As a result I have discovered that a person's destiny, and the fortune they enjoy, is often greatly affected by the powerful spirits that dwell in worlds invisible to the human eye.

This is how things work. Show me someone who is lucky and enjoys tremendous fortune, and I'll show you someone who combines the support of powerful benevolent spirits with genuine hard work and an indomitable will. The real point is to what degree such individual effort can be converted into good fortune, because without that connection – however much the individual might persevere – all their efforts will amount to nothing.

In this book I will detail techniques whereby, through the right approach and frame of mind, you will be able to attract the help of benevolent spirits, and enjoy the spectacular improvements in personal luck and quality of life they can bring about.

To the greatest extent possible, I have avoided any kind of esoteric writing style, and have instead tried to convey my message in an easy-to-understand and practical fashion. As a result, there are areas that I unfortunately have been unable to touch upon, and others which merited a more in-depth study than was given here. I hope at some point in the future to have the opportunity to explain those aspects more thoroughly to my readers.

My only abiding hope is that through a greater appreciation of the spirit world, this book may prove useful to some practical degree in improving the fortunes of as many people as possible.

Toshu Fukami

GOOD FORTUNE
COMES TO
THOSE WHO
ASK FOR IT

The Lucky and the Unlucky

It is possible to distinguish two types of people: there are those people who have good luck and who always seem to find success, and then there are those individuals whose every effort tends to end in failure. When you first look at these lucky people there seems no difference between them and yourself – and yet they manage to enjoy success in everything they attempt, while in your case it seems that things always go wrong just as you feel you are on the verge of success. I think that all of us have experienced this kind of feeling at some time or other.

Faced with your own disappointments and the evidence of other people's success means you can't help but find yourself thinking

'Why is it that he should get all the breaks, when Lady Luck never shows her face at my door?'

And it is these kind of negative doubts and resentments that constantly eat away at those who have experienced repeated misfortune.

In fact, these doubts often lead to people wishing that they too might become lucky – that they too might be able to achieve the happiness and success that good fortune often brings.

And of course it is then understandable that the average person begins to wonder what practical steps they could take to become a luckier person.

Are there really any secrets which can make you a luckier person?

How can you wrap yourself in exceptional good fortune? How is it possible to weed out the seeds of misfortune before they have a chance to grow, or to protect yourself from unforeseen accidents? The answers to these questions are the themes of this book.

I have, over many years of study and practical experience, come to realize that there is a massive invisible chasm separating those who do well at whatever they try and those who don't — and that gap amounts to the adoption, or non-adoption, of certain 'principles'.

As a matter of fact, the disparity in acquiring luck or not doing so can be directly traced to the degree to which an individual bases his behavior on these 'principles'. Anyone who chooses to fully adopt these principles within their everyday lives can easily find themselves blessed with the kind of spectacular good fortune they could previously only dream of.

It should be realized that it is not simply a case of

'He just somehow seems to be lucky.'

If you analyze the situation carefully, you will see that it is actually more a case of

'He does what he has to do to attract good luck.'

I am sure you will find this to be true. If you pay attention to this principle, and then take the time to observe carefully the lives of others, you will find that individuals who have followed this path have succeeded in the vast majority of cases. If you too adopt the idea that you must do what you have to do in order to attract good fortune, you will no doubt soon discover the truth for yourself.

This book will show you how to extract the full potential of your abilities from obedience to these fundamental principles, and the role the spirit world plays in that process. It will introduce you to the 'how to' of actually achieving deep and lasting happiness – all that will remain for you to do is to take the steps necessary to turn those promises into the reality of your own everyday life.

Don't Mope – Just Cheerily Forge Ahead

People who are blessed with good fortune possess a bright core being, and rarely suffer from bouts of depression. Moreover, many of them have a knack of finding something to their advantage in any given situation — they have the ability to say to themselves

'Okay, so even though I have failed this time,
this is still a valuable experience which will help me achieve
significant success the next time around.'

They believe that no matter what the situation, it offers them a springboard to achieving greater future success as individuals. That being so, and odd as it may seem, failures are no longer considered failures, but rather all of them merely represent the 'fertilizer' for future success. Without doubt, successful people, or 'winners', are those people who have overcome the inevitability of past disappointments, and chosen to live their lives according to these beliefs.

Failure is the foundation of success

Being human, when we fail, or when luck chooses to abandon us, we are apt to feel a little down. However, even though we may be feeling this way inside, it is generally unwise for us to reveal these feelings to others in our attitude and words.

Once we say things like

'It's no good, I guess I'm just a loser who never gets a break,'

or

'I feel like it's going to be like this no matter what I do!'

then this kind of attitude invites even worse ill fortune. According to the basic 'schedule of fate', all things work in a cyclical nature, with great success immediately scheduled to follow failure. But if the individual concerned says to himself, 'That's it, kaput!' and throws in the towel, then this schedule is thrown into confusion and the destined time for success is abruptly cancelled.

That being so, when you've experienced some kind of failure and are feeling a little down in the dumps, it's necessary to say aloud to yourself

'It's okay, I'll be fine. It's my destiny to succeed, and to enjoy my share of good fortune.'

If you can find the strength to spur yourself on with your own words you will quickly find your vitality and sense of purpose returning, while in reality you will also be involved in an actual process that invites the forces of good fortune to return to you.

Happiness and good luck don't just come rolling your way out of the blue – the trick is to attract them through a combination of thoughts and actions

If you actively seek out good fortune you will discover that it is surprisingly easy to make contact with it, and to have a happier and more contented life.

If you live a life that is both forward-looking and positive, you will generate the following 'effects':

❶ Your facial expression will brighten, leading to more positive and friendly responses from those you meet.

❷ You will exhibit a positive approach in your words and behavior, leading to a growing attitude that says you can accomplish anything you set your mind to.

❸ Since your circle of friends will grow, you will develop personal skills and good luck when it comes to dealing with people – and better fortune in taking advantage of the opportunities those new friendships may present.

❹ Since you will begin to enjoy the support and friendship of a large number of people, you will also begin to witness steady improvements in the success of both your personal and professional lives.

❺ Life will become increasingly interesting, challenging and fruitful for you.

For all of these reasons, you will discover a feeling of inner happiness — brought about by this highly desirable phenomenon we call 'good fortune'.

The Path to Success: The Cases of the Sumo Wrestler and the Business Tycoon

As I come from Japan, many of my life experiences and the observations I have drawn are from that land. In my country, where the ancient sport of sumo wrestling attracts huge public interest, one of its legendary competitors, Chiyonofuji, also provides us with a fine example of how absolutely everyone is, at some point, given the opportunity to succeed.

 When Chiyonofuji was at the lower *makunouchi* level of the rankings in the world of sumo, he was grouped among the lightweight competitors. However, as he progressed through his competitive career, he matured to the point where his amazing strength and level of technique allowed him to flip over the colossal 250-kilogram wrestler from Hawaii, Konishiki. Indeed, at the peak of his career, aficionados of the sport judged Chiyonofuji to have refined his special style of wrestling to such a level that it could almost be considered an art form. But this was not always the case.

In the early days, and even with his relatively small frame, Chiyonofuji usually attempted to take on his much larger opponents with a straight-on approach. But naturally this put very considerable strain upon his comparatively small shoulders, with the result that on seven separate occasions he managed to dislocate his shoulder, not to mention amassing a catalog of other, less serious injuries. For a sumo wrestler a dislocated shoulder can represent a very decisive handicap, as he never knows when he might dislocate it again, and therefore cannot help in future bouts but be a little hesitant as to whether to commit himself 100 percent.

In the Spring Tournament of 1979, Chiyonofuji threw his right shoulder out once again and had no option but to retire from the contest. As a result, and in line with the Japan Sumo Wrestling Association's rules concerning injured wrestlers, for the next tournament he was demoted from the *makunouchi* level down to the lower *juryo* level – something which represented a humiliating setback to his career. Chiyonofuji was incensed by the decision, and although he was unable to practice fully before he once again came to enter the sumo ring for the next tournament, he still had the skill and good luck to win a majority of his bouts, and was therefore able to achieve what in sumo is considered the remarkable feat of rebounding to the *makunouchi* level after being out for only one tournament.

'Boy, am I lucky!' Chiyonofuji thought to himself. However, he also took this opportunity to change his wrestling style from one in which he sought to grapple with his opponents on even terms into one in which he surged forward and immediately grabbed his opponent's *mawashi*, or waist belt. This became the style he then regularly employed while in his prime, and which led to a career that cemented his legendary status in the world of sumo. Moreover, in order to develop the necessary muscle power, he developed weight-training and exercise programs that became recognized for their effectiveness and complexity as being well ahead of their time.

So although burdened with the great handicaps of being light and prone to shoulder dislocations, Chiyonofuji was still able to climb to the exalted ranks of the *yokozuna* (the highest rank in sumo). Looking at Chiyonofuji's example, it becomes obvious that the good luck that allowed him to rise back to the top ranks after being relegated to the *juryo* ranks for a single tournament was, in the end, the product of a positive attitude, and his own self-generated efforts.

Konosuke Matsushita, founder of one of the world's most successful electronics empires, is another example of someone who was able to make his mark in the world despite three major handicaps: an early life sunk in poverty, a lack of any formal education, and a weak physical constitution.

Let me explain why these 'negative' factors should have become the underlying reasons behind his success.

1. Because of having experienced a young life of desperate poverty, Matsushita was eager to enjoy a lifestyle that was in any way more comfortable than the one he had previously been living.

2. Because of his lack of formal education, he was not bound by any pre-conceived ideas, and subsequently studied twice as hard as the average person in order to overcome his deficiency and learn all he could about management.

3. Because of his own lack of physical strength, he was unable to do all the work that was needed to be done on his own. So, from an early stage of his business, he introduced a system of delegated management, and established a web of subsidiary companies to make tasks like manufacturing and sales more efficient.

The lifestyle environments of these two famous Japanese men, Chiyonofuji and Matsushita, were entirely different – but in both cases their handicaps became the 'fountainhead of their success', and the pattern by which they climbed to the pinnacle in their respective fields was the same. The crucial element was that they were always forward-looking in their attitude, never turning their backs on what fate or fortune had in store for them, but approaching life as a journey full of challenging twists and turns.

Seize the day and make good luck your own!

In a full life, one has to expect failures as well as successes. If you see an opportunity, it is hugely important that you grasp the initiative with both hands, and make good luck your own.

Today is the Day to Seize Your Destiny: The Case of the Baseball Star

Now that we have looked at the cases of Chiyonofuji and the late Konosuke Matsushita, let me turn to the case of Shigeo Nagashima, the former star of Japan's biggest baseball team, the Yomiuri Giants, and explain how he made the sometimes capricious forces of luck work for his benefit.

Even today people still talk about the championship play-off baseball game that took place in 1959 when, with the late Emperor Hirohito in attendance, Nagashima smashed a ninth-inning home run – spectacularly snatching a stunning victory from the jaws of defeat. Nagashima later explained the secret that gave him the ability to deliver regularly when his help was needed most.

On the night before the big game mentioned above, when he went to bed, thoughts of the game the next day filled his head and he used these thoughts to paint for himself a vivid picture of how he hoped the game would play out. He imagined a scene in

which he would hit a home run to the cheers of the crowd present. He further imagined how he would then return home to his wife and children before finally going to bed filled with the rich contentment of victory. After visualizing in thorough detail just how he would behave the next day, and vowing to himself 'I'm sure this is just the way it will happen,' he finally drifted off into a deep and peaceful sleep.

In baseball of course, as in various other sports, mental factors are heavily involved, and in many cases they can make the ultimate difference between victory and defeat. This holds true not only for sport, but also for the world of commerce, where the influence of mental factors can be equally important.

Mental strength is crucial, but if you become tense during those critical moments when it really counts you will be unable to perform to your full potential. On the other hand, if you can relax, you will find yourself able to fully concentrate on the fundamentals, and will be able to fully realize, or on many occasions even surpass what you thought was the extent of your potential.

Furthermore if, besides your own inherent capabilities, you can summon powerful good fortune to your side, you will be able to exert the power of your potential 10 or even 20 times the normal level. To that end, just like Shigeo Nagashima, always think to yourself

'No doubt about it, that is the way it's going to be!'

It is also vital to visualize various aspects and conditions of the situation in minute detail while developing total faith in the final outcome.

If you follow this procedure, when the situation looks difficult, your spirit will retain its strength and you will be able to express your abilities, just as you had hoped.

On the other hand, let us assume that you say to yourself

'Will things really turn out all right? I'm feeling really edgy about this one. I've got a feeling I'm not going to be able to pull this one off.'

Do that and you will have created a strong negative image before things even get underway, and your inner spirit will react by being constantly anxious. As a result, when things come to the crunch you will be so uptight that in most cases you won't be able to help but fail in what you are attempting to do.

In that respect, I believe that Nagashima was quite exceptional in the way he imagined everything down to the smallest detail, even including how he would return to his family a hero and finally go to bed. I think there is little doubt that through this procedure of visualization he was able to attract good fortune to his cause.

So you can see from this example that luck is something that you need to attract to yourself – it is not something that you can be given by somebody else.

___

Heaven helps those who help themselves

___

The first rule is not to forget that you are the one who has to take the necessary steps to attract luck and to thereby become the core nucleus around which the forces of good fortune gather. It is also necessary to develop a proper forward-looking frame of mind toward life, which will encourage you to consistently perform to, or even above, the full level of your inherent capabilities.

If you complete the process needed to beckon luck to your side, then you will discover that these wonderfully positive and beneficial influences will gradually accumulate around you, before enveloping you with all the benevolent force of a great ocean wave.

The important thing is the frame of mind you have at that time. In order to discover just how much good fortune you are now in the position to call forth, you should carefully study the checklist on pages 51 to 56. The more positive action you choose to take, the more certain you are of brightening your personality and making your life more enjoyable.

Another major idea I will be strongly trying to put forward in this book is the concept that if you can manage to bring into play on your behalf power from the spiritual worlds, then you will see the extent of your good fortune increase enormously.

Compared to cases in which latent powers are exhibited as a result of meditation or mental concentration, when power from the spiritual worlds is displayed in a person's life, the power manifested is many times greater.

I have been involved in the study of the spiritual realms since I was in my teens, and as a result, I now know clearly that when people die they become spirits, and that there is a divine world in which the gods live that stands above the spirit world.

Every person has ties with spirits who can bring good fortune to him – his 'guardian spirits'

This book explains what you need to do to encourage the influences of good fortune to be active within your everyday life, viewed from the perspective of a belief in the divine and spirit worlds and the guardian spirits.

In most cases these guardian spirits are high-ranking spirits who are the actual ancestors of the individual in question, from as far back as 10 or more generations. When I refer to their spiritual rank being high, this means that during their lifetimes on Earth they recognized the true value of knowledge and acted in a decent and honorable manner in their dealings with their fellow human beings, and that after their deaths they were appropriately rewarded by moving to high-level spirit worlds. In Japan, in many cases these guardian spirits used to be Buddhist priests, samurai warriors, or scholars — sections of society whose lifestyles were woven with a code which readily corresponded to these high ideals.

In truth it is normal for us to be protected not just by an individual spirit, but by multiple spirits who will be referred to throughout this book as 'guardian spirits'.

FOUR PRINCIPLES FOR ATTRACTING LUCK

1 Go Out of Your Way to
Make Friends with the Lucky

As we go through our lives we are constantly surrounded by friends and acquaintances. If you observe these people carefully, you should be able to differentiate between those who have good fortune as described earlier, and those who don't. A person with good fortune is typically the kind of person who has a strength of will which makes him see everything through right to the end, and yet retains a pretty laid-back attitude throughout. He also tends to be the kind of person his friends would never be able to accuse of being boring, and is instead known for his ready smile and free laughter. If you become friends with this sort of person, then you will improve the quality of your own individual fortune.

On the other hand, the unlucky individual tends to be – how can I put it – gloomy and negative in outlook. You may hear him saying things like

'This is doomed from the start – it's no use even trying.'

Such an attitude means that he never takes the initiative to try to achieve something on his own, while these personality traits also mean it is common for this kind of person to speak ill of others without giving it a second thought. If you end up joining a group made up of this sort of individual, your fortune is certain to take a downturn and any projects you are involved in will probably fail to reach fruition.

What happens then if we take a look at both the person of good fortune and the individual of bad fortune from the standpoint of the spirit world? The person whose fortune is very strong has inevitably surrounded himself with friends whose presence forms a bright whirlpool into which he has willingly been drawn, and in which ultimately he himself occupies the central position. Since this person has adopted a positive approach to all of his actions and endeavors, his guardian spirits have got together and agreed among themselves

'Okay, let's do it. Let's give him our collective backing.'

And they have subsequently adopted a joint stance of total co-operation in helping him out. Consequently, there is no opportunity available for evil spirits to make an appearance, and instead he finds himself constantly surrounded by a positive aura, rich with divine and spiritual benevolence. A further bonus of this help given by the individual's guardian spirits is that these spirits also enlist the help of his friends' guardian spirits, and as a result his good fortune continues to grow and grow. Even in cases where a person experiencing some kind of emotional trauma approaches the lucky individual, then, strangely enough, they too will gain a measure of valuable relief from their pain and find help in quickly regaining their spirits.

The man blessed with good fortune says to himself

'I can probably succeed if I try.'

and then presses ahead confidently with whatever he is trying to do — in other words, he turns his spirit toward the positive and

channels all his feelings in that direction. Conversely, the man of poor fortune sees all around as darkness, and this attitude has a negative effect not just on himself, but on others. Without even acting, he has already envisaged the nature of the results and, true to his predictions, everything turns out unsuccessfully. Even though this kind of person always expects the worst, they are usually also the kind of person who would always consider themselves 'cautious', and tend to remain confident that such an approach is in fact the best one. The limits to this kind of person's understanding is

'You can't expect life to treat you well.'

Because such a person does not live in a forward-looking, positive fashion, his guardian spirits are unlikely to move quickly on his behalf, and consequently he is likely to find his guard weakened when it comes to the attentions of evil spirits. What this usually leads to is the development of personality characteristics in which evil spirits control the individual – and if you become friendly with such a person, you too are likely to come under the influence of destiny orchestrated by evil spirits. People like this are, in an overwhelming number of cases, prone to seeing the worst in others rather than focusing on their good points, and are forever complaining about their family, their job, their situation, or anything else they can think of. Such a person also loses his inner spiritual light – something which shows itself externally in the form of a permanently sorrowful and clouded expression. He seems to be saying to himself

'I'm struggling through this life, carrying all the sorrows of the world on my shoulders, simply trying to survive.'

When dealing with other people or choosing friends, it is necessary to clearly discover whether the other person has the type of personality that is directed by guardian spirits or one whose personality is strongly influenced by evil ones. If you want to help make sure that your fortune turns out as you would wish it to, don't allow yourself to get anywhere near evil spirits, and instead try to come into contact with as many groups of good spirits as possible.

Establish your own existence within a group of benevolent spirits, and your destiny will improve dramatically

---

If at all possible, make up your mind to see your 'circle of good spirits' gradually widen. If you can do this your fortune will dramatically improve, because a soul that encourages the presence of benevolent spirits will, as a consequence, enjoy improvements in things like outlook, clarity and depth of thinking, physical condition, and quality of social networks — all of which factors will combine to establish a strong and distinct movement in the direction of good fortune.

2 Hang Out in Lucky Places

One good method for making the right kind of friends and establishing your own existence within a group of good spirits is to visit religious establishments that are home to powerful benevolent spirits, where you can charge yourself with energy from these spirits.

If you are an individual with well-developed psychic powers, you will know at a glance which places have a highly spiritual atmosphere. Or if you have ready access to a psychic, you can ask about the location of such places.

It is also possible for the average person to discern such things if they really concentrate. It is safest, however, to stay well away from places that seem squalid and where you feel absolutely no stirrings of faith. If you find a place where the air is clear, there is a lot of greenery, and the feeling seems right, then it will probably serve fine. If you pray at such a place, then in most cases your request will be granted.

But let me lay down some criteria for deciding whether a religious establishment is appropriate or not for those people who can tell absolutely nothing from only the atmosphere of a place. I am talking in particular about places where the gods and Buddhas are worshipped in Japan, but the following guidelines can be applied to many religious establishments around the world.

1. The person who performs the religious ceremonies should be sincere and pure-minded.
2. The surroundings and inner grounds should be kept immaculately clean.
3. There should be gravel and other natural surfacing, and there should not be any concrete surfacing.
4. There should be plenty of trees planted in the grounds.

⑤ There should not be any dubious establishments, such as a red-light district, anywhere near the religious establishment.

If a religious establishment does not meet these criteria, or if it does not feel right somehow, then you have to conclude that no higher spiritual essence or good fortune resides there. When the conditions are right, you should feel all the following sensations throughout your being:

① A refreshing 'air' should fill the area.
② It should have a 'developmental' or progressive feeling.
③ A bright atmosphere should prevail throughout the area.

If a place matches the previous evaluation criteria and these rules concerning atmosphere, then you should be able to conclude that it is a place pervaded by strong good fortune, and divine spirits reside there. So when you draw near it, you will feel compelled to pray.

Religious establishments are not the only places where good fortune wells up. Just think of the number of big train stations that you have been to that have a highly developed, prosperous commercial district right in front of the station, but at the back of the station there is a rundown and slightly sinister area. This illustrates the manner in which fortune operates. If you go shopping in the shopping district facing the station, you can make the strong good fortune pervading the area your own.

Quite the opposite is true if you visit the rundown area at the back of the station. There you will experience the following three feelings:

- ✦ dread,
- ✦ a dark atmosphere,
- ✦ an infectious spirit of negativity.

When viewed from the standpoint of the divine and spirit worlds, these areas are revealed to be nests of evil and deceitful spirits, and other unsavory characters from beyond. As with houses that have been abandoned, these areas have been taken over by fox spirits, badger spirits, rat spirits, and other animal spirits. To make matters worse, vicious wanted criminals often lurk here as well. For these reasons, try to avoid entering such areas.

But what happens if you have to go to a religious establishment located in such an undesirable area, say for a friend's wedding? What if, for appearances' sake, you have to pray at such a place? Bear this in mind: if you pray for your own happiness or profit in such a place, you will end up attracting gangs of selfish, evil spirits that will swarm to you, and they will cling tightly to your head, shoulders, stomach, waist, and other parts of your body. You should, therefore, never express your desires if you find yourself in this situation.

If you pray for yourself in a religious establishment located in an unsavory place, you will end up attracting evil spirits to you

---

Instead, it is best for you to pray as follows: 'May this place develop well.' Otherwise, just bow your head and do not wish for anything whatsoever. If you follow this advice, evil spirits will not cling to your person.

As for why such spots should become the dwelling places for evil spirits, it is because they are always running around trying to profit at others' expense. Divine spirits are quickly driven from such places and return to the divine world. And once they have got rid of their betters, the evil spirits then establish squatters' rights. So I implore you to be most careful if you visit a rundown, undesirable area.

3 Organization and Cleanliness Are Keys to Fortune

I strongly encourage those of you who feel that your luck has run out and that fate has dealt you a bad hand, to check your own bedroom or home to make sure everything is spic and span and in its rightful place. At this kind of suggestion no doubt some of you will be feeling skeptical, and saying to yourselves

'Oh, come off it, don't go talking about keeping my room clean. You're beginning to sound just like my mother.'

But strange as you may think, in this particular case your mother really does know best.

Someone who lives in an untidy room every day of his life eventually fails to recognize that the room is, in fact, very messy – he has become used to it to such an extent that his sensibilities have been blunted. However, a person who only occasionally enters that room is certain to think that it is a scene of unpleasant chaos. She might not actually say anything, but she will find it hard to understand the feelings of a person who lives amid such untidiness every single day. That's why your mother in particular would always say, 'This place is a tip, why can't you clean up your room?'

A messy room brings bad fortune, because dirty places are despised by the divine spirits

---

But more significantly, your own guardian spirits dislike untidiness and disorder. Like your mother, they are thinking to themselves 'Why don't you make things a little bit more orderly?' In fact, in these cases the voice of your mother directly corresponds to the voices of your guardian spirits.

There are any number of instances in which people have forfeited good fortune because of the simple fact that their rooms were in a mess.

There at the back of your bookcase is the lottery ticket you bought last year – it might even have been the winner of the $10 million jackpot. Or perhaps you wanted to get in touch with a friend about something important, but were unable to find the piece of paper on which you had jotted down his telephone number. Besides that, you spilled coffee over the book that you were supposed to return to a colleague – and so ended up having to buy a new one as a replacement. Then there is the letter you are trying to write, but there's a word you're not too sure of. So, because you can't find your dictionary among the chaos of your room, you make a rough guess that could turn out to be a big mistake – the choice of a wrong word may mean that the cute guy or girl you are chasing after, or that promising professional contact, might end up actually doubting your intellectual abilities, and your chance will be gone.

If only you had kept your room in proper order, you could have avoided all these problems. But even though you might have missed out on these lucky opportunities, there is no use in crying over spilt milk now. It is better to try thinking of a dirty and disorganized room as a playground for evil spirits, and so if you can discourage these evil spirits from interfering in your life then the chances of you attracting good fortune will be greatly improved.

On the other hand, a clean room is a place where guardian spirits feel comfortable and can enjoy relaxing – and their presence will naturally greatly improve the shape of your fortune. First of all, a clean room makes you yourself feel good, improving your work efficiency by filling you with a vitality and sense of purpose. If you actually look at the spirit worlds, not only is all the 'scenery' and layout breathtakingly beautiful, but everything is also very orderly and systematic. When you look at a tidy room your soul feels refreshed, because somehow your soul is unconsciously aware of conditions in the spirit worlds.

The same applies not only to individual rooms but to the entire home. You should try to keep your home in optimum condition, a step which on its own will lead to a threefold improvement in the extent of your good fortune.

Putting your own room in order and cleaning up the home is a simple strategy for giving a significant boost to your fortune

---

Don't begrudge the labor involved; instead turn your home into one that will make both your guardian spirits and your family happy.

Nor should we overlook the fact that evil spirits tend to gather

in disorderly places. For example, when things are lost or myste-
riously disappear it is often the work of badger spirits, while, like-
wise, malicious fox spirits have a tendency to head for unclean
places looking for the opportunity to hurt or injure people.

HOW ORDER AND CLEANLINESS HELPED
TOYOTA BECOME A MORE POWERFUL COMPANY

Right now in the world of business there is a thriving movement to
improve the work environment in companies, factories, and other
commercial facilities, by eliminating non-essential items or practices. From my point of view this policy amounts to the task of driving out badger and fox spirits, and is a process of which I
readily approve.

There have also been actual cases in which major corpora-
tions have been able to improve their fortunes by promoting a
frame of mind which stresses order and cleanliness – a particularly strong example of which is the world famous Toyota Motor
Corporation. Toyota has been paying a lot of attention to its
'Four S's Movement', a policy initiative designed to improve workplace and management efficiency. The four components of the
program are:

- regulation,
- proper arrangement,
- cleanliness, and
- neatness.

In Japanese, the equivalents of these terms all begin with the sound 's' – hence the name, the 'Four S's Movement'.

No doubt there are some people who find all this a little unusual, saying,

'Is it really possible that simple things like order and cleanliness can truly improve my fortunes?'

The answer to that is an emphatic 'yes'. It is true. Your fortunes can indeed improve in this way. By arranging things logically and keeping everything tidy, by lining up various kinds of tools neatly in an easily comprehensible set-up, they can be readily located when required. As a result, your mind will no longer be occupied by such minor considerations as where a given tool you need might be, leaving you to concentrate fully on the work at hand.

By keeping things clean and tidy you will gain significant improvements in morale across the whole workforce. Furthermore, by eliminating the possibility of rubbish or non-essential objects littering the workplace, there is the added benefit of a significant reduction in the chances of worker injury. But, more than anything else, because you will have created a tip-top working environment, there will be no occasion for useless chatter or time-wasting, something which in itself can lead to radical improvements in efficiency. This creation of a precise working environment is the first step in establishing a *kamban* just-in-time system – the Japanese management style that has become commonly adopted on a world-wide scale.

There is a Japanese saying *ichiji ga banji*. Literally this may be translated as something like 'one thing determines everything,' but it might more freely be translated as 'the child is the father of the man.' This saying is particularly apt for these examples as it intimates that by creating a perfectly ordered workplace, you will also be bringing the same benefits of order and discipline to your own body and soul. Embrace these ideals and good spirits will begin to gather around you, to be quickly followed by tangible improvements in the way your life is heading.

4 Strong Willpower and Vision Will Improve Your Luck 20-times Over

There is another Japanese expression to the effect that a properly shot arrow will pierce and embed itself within the narrow fissure of any rock. Its implied meaning is that if you attack a problem with indomitable will, then nothing is impossible. In Japan there are people who can split chopsticks merely using a business card, or others, such as the karate master Masutatsu Oyama, who are able to break the neck off a beer bottle with a single karate chop. Logically such a feat appears impossible, and yet Oyama does so right in front of your eyes in an example which, if nothing else, reinforces the knowledge that there are many things in this world of ours which remain unexplainable.

Sometimes at the scene of a fire or traffic accident people have witnessed displays of superhuman strength which defy any logical explanation. Many remarkable cases have been well-documented, such as when an American mother, finding her child trapped beneath her burning car after a traffic acci-

dent, was still able to free the child by lifting the car on her own – an object that weighed well over a ton. Such extraordinary feats vividly illustrate the readily acknowledged but logically challenging truth that 'Faith can move mountains.'

Contemporary civilization has conditioned our way of thinking to the point that we often say to ourselves,

'Really, there is absolutely no way such a thing could be possible,'

leading us to forecast the result of our endeavors before we have even made the attempt. But I would point out that the man who splits a set of chopsticks with a business card, or who breaks the necks off beer bottles with his bare hands, never harbors these kind of thoughts. Instead, as he brings down the business card or his hand to strike the blow, he says to himself: 'I am going to cut through. I am already cutting through.' The same goes for the mother of the trapped child. She never thought, 'I can't possibly pick up this car.' Rather she believed at the very core of her soul that she could and would, and so poured every ounce of her strength into the effort.

But in all cases, when the 'impossible' has been made possible, the power of the will – and here I don't mean just the average level of willpower – has been fully harnessed, and the person involved has imagined strongly and in detail the successful outcome of his attempts.

Complete faith is essential for success

If you put your entire being into the resolution to do something, then you will be able to draw upon the spirit power that resides within you, and will therefore be able to achieve astonishing results.

This is not a concept merely limited to esoteric aspects of spiritual and physical power – it also has direct relevance to our daily lives. For example, say you make the firm commitment to yourself

'In the future, I'm going to qualify as a doctor. I'm sure of it,'

and say this to yourself each time you open your textbooks, then there is little doubt that your results in the classroom will begin to improve dramatically. The same thing will happen if you vow to yourself

'I'm convinced of it, I'm going to become the top salesman in my company,'

or

'I am going to enter the Civil Service and follow a career which will make me a valuable asset to my country.'

In such cases, the results will always be 'lucky', because in these kind of instances the forces of good fortune will be drawn toward this feeling of strong resolve, and will thus be encouraged to express their beneficial influence. What this is in essence saying is that 'Complete commitment can be transformed into good fortune.'

If you have a strong idea of what you want the future to hold for you and also possess the resolve to match, the nature of your fortunes will improve 20-fold. Furthermore, if the vision you have is beneficial not just to yourself but to a larger number of people, then its merit is certain to spur numerous guardian spirits into action on your behalf. Sometimes, instead of recruiting an individual's particular guardian spirits to the cause, the forceful extent of the individual's deter-mination will attract other guardian spirits who are more suited by their specific abilities to help him fulfill his goals, and so act as 'substitutes' in place of the former guardian spirits.

The key to this relationship is the nature of the vision of the individual in question, and the strength of that person's will. The strength of willpower will determine an individual's resulting faith in his or her abilities, happiness, and ability to continue to chart out a worthwhile and successful future. The concept of willpower is little more than a combination of perseverance and concen-tration – and is something which reinforces the idea that good fortune is something which you need to carve out for yourself. If you have such faith and willpower, then there can be little doubt that everything you have dreamed of can be ultimately achieved. What's more, many benevolent spirits, beginning with your guardian spirits, will be prompted by the altruistic and heartfelt nature of your desires to come together in forming a strong and united force to help you on your way.

THE RIGHT FRAME OF MIND FOR ACHIEVING SUCCESS

The Family Backgrounds of Those Who Succeed

If you ask society's heros or those who have achieved great success in their lives, about their backgrounds, you will find that in most cases there were at least one or two episodes within their early family life that helped form their characters.

If you gather all these episodes together and carefully consider them, you will discover that there tends to be common threads which link them all – and these shared aspects strengthen the conclusion that there are consistent factors which determine the amount of success and respect an individual is destined to enjoy in society.

Strangely enough, when also viewed from the perspective of the spirit worlds, the conditions under which strong children made it in the world are remarkably like those of episodes in the lives of real heros of society. They include the following

1 Family discipline tends to be fairly strict. The children tend to be very honest and their characters pretty straightforward.

❷ The presence of the mother looms large in the family. Even in hard times, she remains cheerful and optimistic for the future. She tends to think in a constructive fashion and maintains a positive attitude, which becomes a powerful influence in the children's development.

❸ The child is strong in certain fields and feels that he can compete in them alongside others. In other words, although he might not have a particular aptitude for foreign languages or music, he might have a flair for sport or an area of the arts where he feels he can perform with confidence.

The three points above together constitute one major category for achieving success.

Through research it becomes obvious that these children were not 'almighty', but rather that they had at least one area in which they excelled, were always cheerful and optimistic, and retained a respectful attitude toward daily life.

If all of these conditions are fulfilled during the early stages of a child's life, then there is a strong possibility that they will be destined to make their mark in the world.

Greater Dynamism and Heightened Resolution Will Improve Your Luck

'It's no use, I didn't have the right kind of education when I was a child to provide me with the kind of momentum I need to go further in my career. There's no hope!'

Please don't adopt this kind of attitude and give up so easily — even now there are any number of possibilities for improving what the future holds for you. One method would be to improve both your powers of action and your levels of determination. The more a person can enhance his willpower, and can develop firm determination to achieve what he sets out to do, then unquestionably the good fortune that he receives will match the extent of his own efforts. This is because when you have the vision to seize the chances that Heaven provides, then your guardian spirits will team up to support you.

If you think to yourself,

'In the future I am going to become famous and use my position to make a real difference!'

accompanied by conduct which matches your aspirations then, strangely enough, everything that happens in the world around you will seem to be something that is happening for the direct benefit of your own growth and development.

From the spiritual standpoint, it is a person who possesses exceptional determination who appears to be caught up in a surging whirlpool of strong good fortune. So the message here is not to become downcast by small set-backs — if you lift your head up and continue to move forward, your possibilities will improve. Everything gathers strength as it advances forward because an individual's resolution creates a powerful presence in the spirit world.

The Right Frame of Mind Encourages Guardian Spirits To Become Your Friends

There is another important thing to bear in mind.

Human beings have both a physical existence and a spiritual existence. Speaking in broader terms, we all have a 'sixth sense' – the capability to have powerful moments of insight, visions of the future, feelings of *déjà vu* or even telepathic abilities. In other words we are endowed with powers that we all occasionally recognize within ourselves, but which the purely rational process of contemporary science has trouble explaining.

And as a rule lucky people are deeply sensitive when it comes to this 'sixth sense'.

So in other words, if you really want to enjoy perfect good fortune, it is necessary to hone this sixth sense or spiritual power – for control of this sixth sense is a fundamental requirement when it comes to visions of the future, creativity, inspiration to explore the unknown, and other intangible, yet essential ingredients of good fortune. The quickest way to secure this ability is to make your guardian spirits your allies. As I will explain later, you need to hone the spiritual

sense embodied in your *kushimitama* soul (see page 214), and in doing so to promote the right conditions for an optimum sensitivity to our spiritual sense.

Of course, when we are discussing the guardian spirits, we are talking about natural allies. But in order to have the power of the guardian spirits more perfectly reflected in your own fortunes, it is important for you to realize clearly what these guardian spirits are expecting of you, and what is required of you to enable you to come into contact with these same guardian spirits. If you follow the correct procedures, you will be able to discover, and then express, the full level of your innate potential – which of course will meet with a corresponding increase in your ability to attract the influences of powerful good fortune. Your guardian spirits are always there to protect you, and for this reason I urge you to develop a strong awareness that you are being watched over, and that your guardian spirits are your own personal allies.

Be aware that your guardian spirits are your allies and will willingly use their powers on your behalf

---

This is the first step toward drawing on the power of the guardian spirits. I will explain all of this in more detail later in the book.

Treat Your Ancestral Spirits Carefully and Your Family Luck Will Improve

In most cases, your guardian spirits are actually the souls of distant family ancestors. In order to become a guardian spirit, a spirit requires a 'license' in the spirit world. (If a spirit that lacks such a license affixes itself to a living person, then it is instead known as a 'false spirit', an 'evil spirit' or a 'fallen guardian spirit'.)

Until the spirit of a person has been dead for several decades it has not engaged in enough spiritual training in the other world to qualify for such a license.

However, do not take that to mean that such a spirit is devoid of any spiritual power. Such spirits can establish 'temporary abodes' at gravesides and similar locations that are used to commemorate the dead, and then transit back and forth between the spirit and material world, ready to do what they can to protect the safety and health of their living descendants.

Nevertheless, since their level of spiritual awakening (what is commonly referred to as *satori* or 'enlightenment') and wisdom is still of a relatively low level, even though they can lend a certain amount of strength, they in effect function as guardian spirits who can do little in terms of significantly improving the future physical and spiritual progress of their living descendants.

Just as someone who has just acquired a driver's license cannot be expected to be able to operate a car like a professional driver – capable of handling difficult turns and mountain roads with speed and precision – so an inexperienced guardian spirit cannot be expected to guide us through life's unexpected twists and blind corners. After

all, in life we all occasionally have to steer alongside a sheer precipice, and it is at these crucial times that we want to be in the hands of a Class A license-holding guardian spirit.

If the spirits supporting us are not 'licensed guardian spirits', the consequences can be truly disastrous. Yet if we become clearly convinced of the existence of helping spirits imbued with genuine spiritual power, then even if they are not our actual guardian spirits, it would be hugely irresponsible of us to neglect the spirits of our ancestors.

It behoves us to develop a frame of mind in which we treat our ancestral spirits with due care and respect.

Correct Intentions Will Improve Your Luck

As I explained earlier, a high level of determination can directly translate into more powerful good luck – there is, without doubt, a definite direct connection. But what this really boils down to is that strong resolution induces powerful spirits to protect us, and because powerful good luck is brought to us by correspondingly powerful spirits. This is a law of the spirit world.

One principle that you should keep firmly in mind is to make sure that you exercise pure and ethically correct thinking, which you then translate into a positive commitment.

If you think to yourself,

'I would like to have the real strength to bring happiness to others,'

you will receive full marks from the spirit world. However, such altruistic people are not the only kind in this world, and unfortunately there are other people prone to impure thoughts, such as

'I would like to see that guy fall flat on his face,'

or

'I want to kill the bastard!'

Such an evil train of thought also has reverberations in the spirit worlds, where evil spirits who are attuned to this kind of thinking quickly gather around such people.

If a person has negative, hate-fuelled intentions, then the fortunes of both him and the object of his grudge will decline drastically

---

There is a Japanese proverb the meaning of which is 'Putting a curse on someone is a two-edged sword,' and it happens to ring very true in these cases. If a person is completely unhappy while in the material world, then after he dies and enters the spirit world his destiny dictates that he will continue to be weighed down by his grudges, and will suffer greatly as a result. Consequently, the most important thing is to nurture correct and decent thinking so as to be able to inspire the spirit worlds and to call forth good fortune.

If you strive your hardest 'for the sake of the world and for the sake of my fellow human beings,' a host of good spirits, beginning with your guardian spirits, will lend you their support.

Your good deeds will be acknowledged by the spirit world and you will find yourself showered with good fortune in return

---

When I talk about enlisting the power of the spirits, it is important that you do not consider this to be anything related to the occult – rather it is the ability to demonstrate the power of the spiritual world within your daily life. It would be wise to caution you not to be mistaken in this respect, as even high-class spirits could take offence at such a mistaken assumption.

Bathe Yourself in the Energy of Your Lucky Star

Another method that anyone can employ to improve his fortune is to harness the energy of his 'lucky star'. No doubt many readers are astounded by this statement and are saying to themselves, 'What kind of nonsense is he talking about!' However, if you are willing to alter the emphasis of your consciousness just a little, it can become possible to be bathed in the incredible energy which comes from the stars – and is something which in turn could be linked to improving your fortune.

The first thing to bear in mind here is that the stars are not simply lumps of matter: rather, just like we human beings have our spiritual worlds, so too do the stars. I would like you to understand that the stars are wrapped in their own 'spiritual aura', and are constantly giving off material and spiritual energy that radiates to the Earth. The fact that mankind has a long and illustrious history of employing horoscopes and related techniques to predict our fates is proof that the stars have a very significant spiritual existence, which exerts a major influence upon us all.

So here we should seek to move forward a step or two in the development of our consciousness, so as to be able to expose our entire being to the positive energy coming from the stars.

Discussion upon the merits of divination, fortune telling, or similar techniques can now be considered largely redundant. In today's hectic world it is up to you to actively beckon good fortune to your side by seeking empathy with your own lucky star. If you gaze at the sun, the moon, and the other celestial bodies stretching across the sky with an open mind and an open heart, then the tiny insignificance of your own physical existence will soon melt into a feeling of oneness with the vastness of the universe. As a result, when it comes to your relationship with the stars, your

perception will alter radically, such that instead of considering stars as things 'to see', you will think of yourself as being seen by, protected by, led by, and deriving power from those very same stars. Your previous lack of empathy with the cosmos will come to an end and instead you will discover that, by bathing yourself in the energy of the stars, you will improve your fortune, and induce your guardian spirits to work harder on your behalf.

In addition, if you choose to employ the hugely powerful 'spirit world good luck logos' – explained in Chapter 5 – as you are developing this celestial connection with the stars, you will multiply your good fortune many times over. I cannot recommend strongly enough that you employ this consciousness-adjusting technique – and through it seize the chance to shape your destiny to bring you happiness, success, and good fortune.

Perplexing Choices or Decisions Offer Chances for Success

There are many occasions in life when we are forced to make choices as to what we should do. There are so many choices in life – everything from which shoes to buy in the sale to what career path we should pursue. Although the degree of importance of each decision might vary, every day we are presented with a bewildering number of choices and decisions.

A lucky person will consistently choose the right direction – while a luckless person will tend to get caught in a quandary before making, after much anguish, a choice which ultimately proves to be the wrong one. If that mistake in choice is an insignificant one then it may merely provoke some laughter, but there are other times when mistaken choices can threaten to ruin an entire lifetime.

'Oh my God! Which one should I choose?' Up until this point everyone is in the same boat, wondering what to do. But depending on the way the person facing the decision is thinking at that moment, he will either make the correct choice or instead make a choice that will send him down the wrong road.

In the case of a person who makes the right choice, his way of thinking will be something like this:

'I have done everything I can on my own, so from this point on, I will trust Heaven to decide my fate. However, since I have the gods of good fortune on my side, I'm sure it'll be the right choice. This is my destiny. But even if it doesn't quite work out as I plan I still intend to have no regrets.'

As for the person who makes the wrong choice, he will say something like this to himself:

'What on earth am I going to do if I get this wrong? I'm going to be in a total mess. I'm always so unlucky that I'm bound to make the wrong decision this time too ...'

It's a pity, but that's just the way it is.

So in other words, individuals who have powerful good fortune also possess a strong sense of faith and firmly believe that things will, 'without fail', turn out in a certain way. Such adamant faith also serves to attract powerful good fortune to their side, while the situation for ill-fated people is, unfortunately, the complete opposite.

> It is apparent that the a person's frame of mind is paramount in influencing the shape an individual's destiny takes

Furthermore, if you use this optimistic frame of mind as the base and then utilize the power both of your guardian spirits and the stars of the cosmos, you will experience the joy of seeing your fortune improve before your very eyes.

So, especially on occasions when you are perplexed as to a choice or decision, I would urge you to consider these ideas as a chance for you to greatly improve your fortune.

A CHECKLIST FOR BRINGING A GREAT TRANSFORMATION IN YOUR FORTUNE

You can determine your own lucky fortune levels
using the checklist below.

Yes = 3   Average = 2   No = 1

[3 2 1]	1	My personality is bright and cheerful.
[3 2 1]	2	I don't tend to worry very much.
[3 2 1]	3	I hate fighting and like to get along with my friends.
[3 2 1]	4	If someone is having difficulties, I try to help them.
[3 2 1]	5	I feel uncomfortable around people who are behaving badly.
[3 2 1]	6	I am fond of animals, and enjoy taking care of them.
[3 2 1]	7	I take a positive approach toward everything I do.
[3 2 1]	8	If someone makes a mistake, I forgive them quickly.
[3 2 1]	9	I listen to the opinions of others.
[3 2 1]	10	Even if not beneficial to me, I will keep on working for other people in order to complete a project.
[3 2 1]	11	If someone asks me for directions, I like to make sure I give clear and accurate instructions on how to get there.
[3 2 1]	12	I always give up my seat to an elderly person on the bus or train.

Good Fortune Comes to Those Who Ask for It

[3 2 1]	13	When I'm happy, I show it.
[3 2 1]	14	I show respect to my colleagues.
[3 2 1]	15	I truly believe that failure is the mother of success.
[3 2 1]	16	I try to focus on the strong points of people, rather than their weak points.
[3 2 1]	17	I clearly express my thoughts.
[3 2 1]	18	I enjoy making people laugh.
[3 2 1]	19	I faithfully keep my promises.
[3 2 1]	20	I always finish what I start.
[3 2 1]	21	If I realize I am in the wrong, I apologize without hesitation.
[3 2 1]	22	I say 'yes' more often than I say 'no'.
[3 2 1]	23	I believe that I am a happy person.
[3 2 1]	24	I treat younger members of the family and children gently.
[3 2 1]	25	I have a large circle of friends.
[3 2 1]	26	I love my parents and grandparents.
[3 2 1]	27	There are a lot more people I like than people I dislike.
[3 2 1]	28	I like to praise the strong points of other people.
[3 2 1]	29	I always keep my workdesk and bedroom neat and tidy.
[3 2 1]	30	If someone asks for my help, I like to cooperate with them as much as I can.
[3 2 1]	31	I am not a fussy eater, and enjoy most foods.
[3 2 1]	32	I make sure to always wear clean clothes.
[3 2 1]	33	I love the words 'courage', 'love', and 'sincerity'.
[3 2 1]	34	I like to think in terms of improving things.
[3 2 1]	35	Even when something unfortunate happens, I think in positive terms of overcoming the problem.

[3 2 1]	36	I can still get on with people I do not particularly like.
[3 2 1]	37	I always want to be the best.
[3 2 1]	38	I hate to lose.
[3 2 1]	39	I always take care with matters of importance.
[3 2 1]	40	I feel convinced that the world will not come to an end.
[3 2 1]	41	I feel certain that divine and spirit worlds do exist.
[3 2 1]	42	I believe that people are rewarded for their efforts.
[3 2 1]	43	I believe that the world has more good people than bad.
[3 2 1]	44	I never forget other people's generosity.
[3 2 1]	45	I carefully consider warnings or advice offered by other people.

How to Evaluate the Fortune Transformation Checklist

I believe that the world is full of people who at this very moment are concerned about how lucky they are. This is because they believe that if they were fully aware of how lucky they are, they would be able to react more positively to things that they encounter, value themselves properly, and (to a certain extent) exert control over their situation.

Blindly charging ahead in the face of bad luck is an exercise in futility, whereas if your fortune is bright, although you should still approach things cautiously, being armed with the knowledge that you are lucky enables you to deal with the situation in a confident and resolute manner.

With the above checklist, you can perform a quick spot check on the conditions related to your own fortune. If your score is low, and it is clear that you have a 'tendency toward poor fortune', reflect carefully upon your deficiencies before making a new start.

On the other hand, if your score is high, proceeding with over-confidence bordering on arrogance will simply trip you up and invite unmitigated failure. It is important therefore to always maintain an attitude that, while recognizing your abilities and confidence, still remains essentially humble.

Good fortune is not something you receive from anyone else, it is something you create yourself. Never forget, however, that you do have the ability to call it to yourself. Another point concerning this checklist which needs to be addressed is that even if your score on the checklist is poor, you should not abandon hope and consider yourself a lost cause — for the instant those negative thoughts take control your destiny really will take a turn for the worse. Instead, in those moments when everything seems without hope it is best to think to yourself

'My luck can't get any worse than this. From here on, I'm going to turn it around.'

Do that and your spirits will quickly brighten, and your situation will gradually begin to improve.

I would like you to evaluate your scores on the checklist with these points in mind.

Scoring and Evaluation

Each 'yes' is worth three points; each 'average' two points; and each 'no' one point. Choose your answer in accordance with how you truly react to each statement.

120 POINTS OR MORE

You are already the beneficiary of great fortune – now all you have to do is continue to maintain, or even improve, certain aspects of your behavior. If you abandon the ego and increase your strength of determination you have the potential to become a person of prominence and someone in tune with the spirit of the age.

100 TO 119 POINTS

You are close to enjoying very good fortune. If you positively involve yourself in good deeds, possibly through voluntary work or similar selfless acts, while also making positive steps to be better welcomed by other people, you will be able to further improve your level of good fortune.

70 TO 99 POINTS

You have to abandon your selfish way of thinking, and instead strive to live a life which brings happiness, not just to yourself, but to others. If you wish to attract better fortune, do not forget to be aware of, and to nurture, the valuable spirit of gratitude.

69 POINTS OR LESS

If you leave things as they are, there is a very real danger that you will attract the presence of evil spirits and subsequently see your fortunes decline very rapidly. First of all, spend time reflecting on the way you live your life, and quickly begin to start giving due and proper respect to others. Start living in the correct spirit, avoid needless confrontations, and adopt a more cheerful frame of mind to help revive your fortunes.

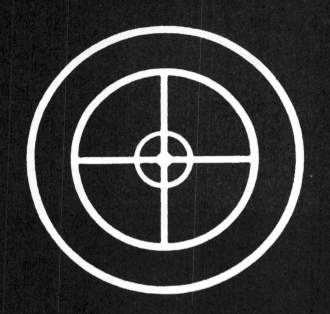

ANOTHER YOU WHO
CAN PRODUCE EITHER
GOOD FORTUNE OR
POOR FORTUNE

Guardian Spirits – The Case of the *Manga* Artist

Up to this point I have talked quite extensively of guardian spirits, but I suspect that there are still some readers who find it difficult to envisage exactly what I mean. So rather than draw a sketch of a guardian spirit by myself, I will instead allow my hand to be used by a guardian spirit to produce their own self-portrait. In providing a specific example of this, let me explain the case of the renowned *manga* artist Reiji Matsumoto. *Manga*, the Japanese comic books, enjoy huge popularity in my country as do the artists responsible for their creation. At the end of 1985 Reiji Matsumoto, recognized as one of our greatest living *manga* artists, visited our offices to join in an 'investigation' into the nature of his guardian spirits and an exploration of his previous lives.

On the day in question, in addition to Matsumoto there were also several people from a publishing company present. It was a crisp, sunny day quite a few years ago, but all of us still clearly remember the fascinating manner in which we eventually learnt the truth about Matsumoto's guardian spirits, and the extent of his previous lives.

I sat down facing Matsumoto, concentrated all my energy and thoughts into that one moment, and then entered into a trance which gave the divine spirits full freedom to enter my body.

'I can see them now!' I said. 'It's amazing Reiji, I can see that you are accompanied by what appears to be a total of 69 guardian spirits. And the chief one among them is this character.'

While speaking I experienced the sensation of the whole of my body warming – a phenomenon caused by the strong spiritual force that had taken over my body. With this I began to draw, on the sketch book in front of me, the face of the prominent figure I had noticed among the guardian spirits. In reality, it was not me who was drawing the picture, but rather the guardian spirit who had taken over my body and was now sketching its own self-portrait – something which meant that, as a result, there was very little deviation from the true appearance of the spirit. As my hand skipped across the paper, I also carried on an interior monolog. 'Is that right? It should be this way here. The ears should be about this long. The beard is a little fuller, isn't it?'

As I neared completion of the picture, I became more and more relaxed, which was followed by an overwhelming sense of joy that gradually enveloped me. As my hand put the finishing touches to the picture and as, in my excitement I got a little ahead of myself, the guardian spirit would give me specific suggestions, such as 'a little bit shorter there' or 'darker there'. Judging by the spiritual vibrations he gave off, he was a very illustrious individual.

About five minutes after I had begun drawing, we had a completed picture of a man's face there on the paper in front of us. All that remained to be added were the eyes and the name of the actual 'artist' who had guided my hand.

Once the final pieces of the picture had been added we were surprised to discover that Matsumoto's chief guardian spirit was Keikoh, the 12th Emperor of Japan who, according to legend, was born in the first century of the Christian era.

According to early records Keikoh was the father of the legendary Japanese hero Yamato Takeru no Mikoto, who is said to have been the conqueror of the Kyushu region (one of the main islands of Japan). The realization quickly came to me that this was probably why Matsumoto had been inspired to produce his immensely successful *manga* strip *Space Warship Yamato*, in which the heroic crew battles its way through numerous difficulties until finally completing its mission. I got the strong feeling that everything that Yamato Takeru no Mikoto's life symbolized was somehow connected to this series of comic stories.

After Emperor Keikoh had finished his self-portrait, the guardian spirit began to convey messages through me about Matsumoto. He intimated how he had been protecting Matsumoto since the age of 17, and how he intended to continue watching over Matsumoto in the hope that he would see all the dreams of his youth finally fulfilled.

As these messages were passed to me I found my own curiosity being aroused, and naturally wanted to ask Matsumoto my own questions about events of the past. But before I got the chance I was suddenly overcome by overwhelmingly dark spiritual vibrations that sat, it would be best to describe, like some heavy presence upon my chest. It was an extremely depressing feeling, which was immediately accompanied by a spirit's voice that began to speak in a low, quivering tone. 'Damn you Emperor, damn you.' He kept repeating this same phrase over and over again. Obviously this spirit had a deep hatred of some emperor, but I was confused by the way that when he spoke, he used the term for a non-Japanese emperor. Who on earth could the person speaking be, I asked myself.

We all held our breaths and waited for developments as one, two, and then three minutes passed. As the seconds ticked by, I continued to draw pictures of this other previous incarnation of Matsumoto for all I was worth. As I did this I was in deep discomfort, with a feeling as if my entire body had been drained of blood, while the people around me bore witness as my face became pale, and my lips dry.

I was being tormented by the question of what on earth could have happened during one of Matsumoto's previous incarnations?

By now around five minutes had passed and the picture I was drawing was nearing completion. I was just finishing the part around the eyes, and as I drew the forehead I could detect extremely powerful thought-waves emanating from that area. As the picture from a previous existence came into final shape, we could all clearly see a face filled with anger.

'Who could this possibly be?' I thought to myself. In answer the spirit borrowed my right hand and wrote: 'Sima Qian.'

What a shock! In a previous life Matsumoto had been the illustrious Chinese historian Sima Qian, writer of the *Annals of the Grand Historian*.

I explained: 'From his appearance I can tell that, for a long period of time, Sima had been confined in a dark, narrow space before finally being put to the sword. It seems that Sima carries a deep hatred of Emperor Han Wudi, whom he holds responsible for his dreadful fate.'

As always when I have given such explanations, this power with which I am able to see the previous lives of people

(often referred to as 'subconscious simultaneous interpreta-
tion' or 'the subconscious power to see the hearts of others')
left me mentally drained, and so with a sigh I gratefully sank
back into the welcoming softness of my office couch.

'You mean to say that Sima Qian was a prior incarnation of
myself? Wow, I simply never would have dreamed of that. I
feel weak at the knees.'

Matsumoto's eyes were filled with happiness although,
perfectly understandably considering the nature of the rev-
elations, there was still an element of doubt in his mind.

I explained to him that Sima Qian had already been
reborn twice in the past, so that Matsumoto actually represented his third reincarnation. I also noted that memories
from when Sima was alive still existed inside Matsumoto,
although strictly speaking, Sima Qian and Matsumoto were
not the 'same individual'. Even so, Sima continued to dwell
in the subconscious memories lodged in the depths of
Matsumoto's brain.

As we talked more and got to know each other better, I learned
that Matsumoto was strongly interested in ancient civilizations
and historical relics — something which added weight to the suggestion that the thoughts of Sima Qian from a previous existence
had taken form inside Matsumoto, and been translated within his
present existence into a romantic interest in ancient history.
Upon further study of his *manga* comics it became apparent that

within his work, Matsumoto has a pronounced tendency to show his personal feelings of like or dislike for various historical figures, and to draw very clear distinctions between good and evil. When we compared the known personality characteristics of Sima with those of Matsumoto, we were astonished to find that they were a perfect match.

So this example of one of Japan's contemporary heros shows us how we can often see that people develop a passion in a certain area, or feel that Heaven has set them on a certain career path, because of thoughts transmitted to them through previous incarnations.

It Is Fine to Make Requests of Your Guardian Spirits

Perhaps you are the kind of person who thinks that, as your guardian spirit can see everything – even within the deepest recesses of your soul, when asking for help about something there is no need to make your request out loud. True enough: at the instant your guardian spirit gazes into your mind he can see immediately the exact content of your desires.

However, it is also important to remember that guardian spirits were originally human beings too, just like you or I, and so if you politely address your guardian spirits out loud, communication will be easier and the spirits will be pleased by the way you make your appeal vocal. The situation here is analogous to what happens when a child asks a parent for something. Just the look on a child's face or the way she acts will usually give parents a good idea of what toy their daughter really wants — and if with big, sparkling eyes she pleads for something, it has to be a pretty cold-hearted parent who has the strength to refuse her.

Children will fidget and put on little shows when they want something. The father might be standing there in a quandary, wondering to himself, 'I wonder if I should buy it for her. Oh, what should I do?' And then, excitedly, the little girl will say, 'Daddy, buy that for me pretty please!' And, thinking to himself, 'Well, if she really wants it that badly, let's get it for her,' the father will probably reach for his money.

Just think of yourself as that child, and your guardian spirit as the parent, because your relationship with your guardian spirit is very much like that between child and parent. Another important thing to bear in mind when seeking help from your guardian spirit is that, if you do put your wish into words, they become what is known as *kotodama* or 'words with a soul of their own'. These words, imbued with their own power, in turn stimulate energy from your subconscious, which deepens your own spiritual confidence in your guardian spirit when you come to make your request.

Unlikely as it may sometimes seem, if you say something like the following, you will immediately gain a greater sense of confidence within yourself:

'Guardian spirit, grant this request ... let my good fortune increase 10-times over.'

In return, your guardian spirit will probably reply,

'Since you have spoken up and asked me for this wish, it shall be granted,'

which, incredible as it may sound, will suffuse your body with a feeling of even greater confidence.

Be as precise and clear as possible when framing your wishes, enunciate each word clearly as you ask for help

---

Expressing your requests in such a concrete and clear fashion will make the response to your wish speedier and more authoritative. For example, take the following request as a model.

'Guardian spirit, tomorrow from one to two in the afternoon, I have to go over the monthly estimates with the Marketing Manager. Could you do your utmost to create the right conditions so that he and I can reach easy agreement. Then at 3:30 p.m. I have to meet Sarah in the library – she wants

Lucky Fortune

me to give her and her fiancé some advice before they get married. Please make sure that I don't err in what I say, and that my advice may be instrumental in ensuring that the two of them enjoy a happy life together.'

I think you can see what I am getting at here – the point is to be as detailed as possible when it comes to the names of the other people involved, the place, the time, the specifics of the relationship, and the exact outcome you are hoping for.

Let your thoughts contain the idea that you wish the best for the other people involved as well as for yourself, and let your words show that you are determined to improve yourself, even as they express confidence and thanks for the actions that your guardian spirit is going to take on your behalf. If when you make your requests you put deep and sincere feeling into your thoughts and words, then the chances are very good that you will receive just about everything you ask for.

However, there will still be cases in which no matter how much you ask your guardian spirit, your wishes fail to be granted. Why should this be so?

First of all, there is the possibility that your frame of mind is wrong. You are being overly conceited, arrogant, careless, lazy, or are of some similar mind-set that is considered unworthy by your guardian spirit. In such cases, your attitude will only serve to alienate your guardian spirits, with the unfortunate result that no matter how much you pray, it will have absolutely no effect.

Next, you may be too desperate to see the outcome you desire. In which case your obvious desperation will cause dark clouds to gather around you, and so your guardian spirits will be slow in moving to help you.

Finally, your guardian spirits will only grant those requests which they feel will bring happiness not just to yourself, but to the other people involved.

There are ways to avoid the problems involved here, as indeed there are other frames of mind in addition to the ones specified above that will alienate the guardian spirits. But regardless of the nature of the obstacle that may be hindering the guardian spirits' willingness to help, there is one good way to ease the process: pour all of your heart into the end of your prayer, and make sure to complete it by saying, 'Oh, guardian spirit, *I now entrust everything to you.*'

Human beings are unaware of what course their lives will take and whether they will be filled with sadness, happiness, or (as in most cases), a constantly changing combination of the two. Consequently, they are often tormented by the uncertainty of their lives and tend to become fixated on immediate results. However, since the guardian spirits exist within the spirit world, they have the ability to see what lies in store for us far, far into the future. This means that they are fully aware that the things you are asking for now may not always be in the interests of your long-term happiness.

The depth of your desire to see your wishes fulfilled is fundamentally important in seeing them come true

---

As a rough measure it is fair to say that 80 percent of your potential to see your wishes fulfilled depends on your total belief when you make your request – the remaining 20 percent should be left to your guardian spirits' evaluation of the situation, taking into consideration their ability to view the future.

So long as you remain aware of these issues and modify your behavior accordingly, then your life will take a positive path – as long as you retain firm resolve and determination. At those times, especially, when everything seems to be heading in exactly the opposite direction than you had intended, leave matters to your guardian spirit, and think to yourself

'This shows that my guardian spirits are looking deeply into the future, and have obviously decided that what I have asked for is not good for me in the long term. So no matter how many times I keep asking for it, it appears that my fate is destined to move in the opposite direction. I now feel confident the course they have chosen is the best for me in the long run, so I must abandon my stubborn desire to move in the other direction and instead embrace this road and all it has to offer. It seems a little difficult to understand your motives at this particular moment, guardian spirit, but I fully trust you to know that this is the correct course for me to take in the long term.'

Replies Come via Your Dreams and Intuition

Well then, how exactly will your guardian spirits respond to your requests? Let us take a specific example. Say you have received your Christmas bonus and are in a quandary as to how to spend it – should you take your family for a holiday in the sun, or should you purchase that stereo you have your heart set on? In such a situation, it is best to make an appeal to your guardian spirits in the following way:

'Guardian spirits, please tell me what would be the best choice for myself and my family.'

This can probably be characterized as the normal way to seek guidance. If you are a person who has undergone some form of spiritual training, when you close your eyes as you make your request, you might in that instant see a scene inside your head in which you and your family are seated around the living room enjoying crystal-clear music coming from the stereo. Or alternatively, you might have a vision where you and your family are having the time of your lives in some sun-drenched, exotic resort. Such images are the response of the guardian spirits to your question, although it must also be admitted that cases of such instant response tend to be relatively few.

More commonly, we have cases in which the guardian spirits choose to make their reply within the framework of dreams. In such cases, even a person who does not normally have clear dreams will, on that night, form distinct images in his sleep: images, for example, of him and his family engaged in pleasant conversation on a plane, or of standing in a record shop looking at CDs. In such cases, the dreams will be in color and will be very vivid, such that the person will remember the details as he awakes, and after waking up will leave him with a pleasant 'after-taste' he will be reluctant to give up.

Conversely, if a guardian spirit wants to tell you the idea of a trip is a bad one, he will have you see a dream in which there is a plane or train crash, or some kind of similar catastrophic situation. In effect, what he is doing is giving you a warning signal, which it would be wise to heed by giving up the idea of the trip.

The Answer Might Also
Come through Those Around You

When it comes to dealing with a highly rational, serious-minded person who has little capacity for intuition and places no significance in dreams, the guardian spirits kindly try a different approach. After listening carefully to your requests, they will attempt to convey an answer to you in an indirect fashion, which is usually repeated on at least three occasions. This is because if the answer is given only once or twice the person will usually either simply not notice it or choose to dismiss its significance. So in order to ensure the enlightenment of individuals who find it difficult to recognize signs from the spirit world, the guardian spirits make a practice of replying three times or more.

Let me give a specific example.

The first attempt your guardian spirits make to contact you may sometimes take the form of a sun-tanned old friend you bump into on the street, who then proceeds to talk in glowing terms of the recent trip he and his family all enjoyed in the Mediterranean. Even though you may not be paying much attention as he rambles on, if you are reasonably attuned to the spirit world you may quickly realize, 'That's it! He has been sent as a messenger from my guardian spirits!' – and at that very moment you will make up your mind to spend your bonus on a family trip.

However, there will be some people who will fail to recognize the significance of such a meeting, and to whom the guardian spirits will make a second approach.

Again it comes out of the blue. This time the telephone suddenly rings. It's a call from your parents who, during the conversation, mention a friend who has recently bought a villa in the south of France, and who is inviting people to visit him. In this manner, or in some even less direct fashion (such as you opening up the daily newspaper to find a rash of articles on the regions around the Mediterranean), the spirits will help direct you toward the correct decision.

The vast majority of people are by now likely to feel that their guardian spirits are at work and decide to take the family on a holiday in the sun.

However, in order to get the message through to the few people who still remain oblivious to these signs, guardian spirits will try a third and final approach. They will make the greatest of efforts to try to win over the last doubters who refuse to recognize the significance of all these coincidences.

On the third approach, a salesman suddenly shows up at your front door and rings the bell.

'Excuse me, I am your guardian spirit.'

Well no, of course he doesn't really say that literally. But this particular salesman just happens to be a travel agent who likes to sing the praises of holidays in the Mediterranean. For a moment you wonder to yourself since when did travel agents start making door-to-door sales calls – but before you know it you are carried away by his smooth sales talk, and it is only after you have put down a payment for a holiday on the Côte d'Azur that you finally realize, 'Of course, that was the answer I was looking for from my guardian spirit!'

If a person's intuition is sometimes lacking, his guardian spirits will still seek to get their message to him through dreams, through the words of his friends or acquaintances, or even through the visits of direct emissaries

---

If all these approaches still fail to impart the message you can just imagine the pitifull state of those frustrated guardian spirits! Actually that is not so, since from the point of view of the guardian spirits this thick-skinned attitude has a very positive dimension. Repeated instances of questioning followed by doubts can lay the basis for real faith — for without a number of serious tests the edifice of faith can be too easily destroyed.

This is especially true when a person is standing at a cross-roads in their life. It may seem an imposition to have one's guardian spirits work so hard to convey their will, but if a person deeply and repeatedly questions his faith, then the conviction that this fre-quent testing promotes will be translated into (and be ultimately proven by), that person's actions. So that is why guardian spirits are more than happy to make the necessary efforts.

Moreover, if people rely too much for life's choices on direct intuition and dreams then they run the risk of too often taking for granted that their wishes for the future will come true. This, in turn, can lead to damaging psychological instability. Furthermore, because of their penchant for mischief, evil spirits enjoy making use of both intuitive responses and indirect evidence – which altogether means that great care needs to be taken in interpreting messages correctly.

Making Big Problems Smaller and Smaller Problems Go Away

If your question is a direct one, such as how to use your money or where to move to, and you get a direct answer in return, then you can move forward in life with confidence. But unfortunately there will be cases where disasters are simply unavoidable and where even your guardian spirits can do nothing whatsoever to help you.

When Heaven sees the need for a personal disaster in order to spur an individual on to greater personal growth, such a situation is inescapable. Certainly Heaven does not place these disasters in our way with evil intentions, but rather it does so with a heavy heart and solely for the benefit of the development of the person himself. In such distressing cases it is sadly true that it is probably best just to grin and bear it.

However, there are also cases in which evil spirits inflict serious mishaps on people just for spite. For example, they might cause you to become ill or suffer an injury, or they may even cause you to have an accident just as you were about to successfully complete some deal – leaving you frustrated and empty-handed. At these times not only do you find yourself facing a major setback but, if you're not very careful, you might also find yourself on the slippery slope of continuing misfortune. It is now that you quickly need to do something to salvage the situation.

What is really required is for us habitually to ask the help of our guardian spirits before such a disastrous situation can develop in the first place. Furthermore, since we can never know when we might meet with an unfortunate accident, we should appeal to our guardian spirits every day for their protection, especially when our lives are filled with relatives and family members who might be the target of evil spirits.

Does that mean that we are to treat our guardian spirits as hired bodyguards? Yet these are bodyguards who don't actually get paid. Are we to consider the existence of these guardian spirits as being a valuable freebie – for which we have no need to pay any bonuses, social security, unemployment insurance or the like – and think of them as personal attendants who work for us, without a break, pay or protest, 24 hours a day, 365 days a year?

It is necessary to have very genuine feelings of gratitude toward your guardian spirits. If you have such honest feelings, then in your guardian spirits you will find allies whose help and generosity it would be impossible to overvalue or replace

---

You should say to yourself: 'Guardian spirits, please watch over me. Sorry, I realize that you are already watching over me, but just hope you can maintain your vigilance, for which I'm truly grateful.'

Moreover, the stronger your faith becomes, the stronger becomes the power exerted by your guardian spirits on your behalf. Aided by it, you can minimize the effects of the disasters into which you fall, so that major disasters in which you were originally destined to find yourself enmeshed become minor disasters, while minor disasters no longer fall within your path.

This approach works not only with the mischief perpetrated by evil spirits — it can also sometimes alleviate the severity of the spiritual trials to which you are put by Heaven. In other words, your guardian spirits will lobby Heaven on your behalf, saying, 'Since he is really trying, please go a little bit easy on him with this one.' In such a situation the severity of the spiritual test might be reduced from the equivalent of 100 points down to something closer to 80 points. In essence, what it boils down to is, if individuals have a genuine desire to really change their behavior and to make wholehearted efforts to improve their spiritual condition by working to improve the world we live in, then Heaven will be willing to listen to the appeals of guardian spirits made on their behalf.

Your Own Efforts Are Essential

In persuading your guardian spirits to listen to your requests, it's important to bear in mind that if you neglect to do what you are supposed to do, the resulting price you have to pay may be heavy.

Let me take this opportunity to recount a bitter-sweet personal experience of mine which ably illustrates this point, and which happened when I was a university student.

Examination time was fast approaching, but I knew I hadn't studied nearly enough. I would sit down at my desk with my books open, determined to really make a go of it – but for some reason I just couldn't concentrate. I guess my mind was still preoccupied with the duties surrounding my heavy involvement in a number of university societies. As I sat at my desk I was getting increasingly frustrated by my inability to study, and so finally ended up imploring the gods and my guardian spirits for their help. 'Now you're going to get the hang of it,' I said to myself, as I set about studying once more with rekindled motivation.

Sure enough, I seemed to get one brainstorm after another regarding what questions would appear on the test papers. These brainstorms, although hugely valuable of course, were still not enough to cover every aspect of the exam, so I had to continue studying frantically long into the night. Then came the time for the exam itself. How did I do? To my delight, the inspirations I had that night directly corresponded to many of the questions written on the paper, as well as providing useful insights into areas which, although insufficiently covered by the text books, appeared on the exam paper as well. I was delighted to later discover I had earned the top mark in the class!

Upon getting my results I thanked my guardian spirits in a somewhat selfish manner: 'Those brainstorms of mine were great. I'm sure you guardian spirits showed me the answers. Help me out the next time as well, won't you?' I said.

Well, now it was several months later and the exam season was coming round again. This time I was not all that worried – the reason being that I figured my study mates, my guardian spirits, would see me easily through. In fact, I was brimming with confidence in the knowledge that I would again receive the inspiration when it was needed, and just as I expected, when I closed my eyes I could vividly see the examination questions floating there in my mind. There I was, saying to myself: 'So these are the questions that are going to appear on the test this time around. I see, I see.'

Exam day finally arrived and I sat there at my desk, eager to receive the question papers. I was nearly bursting with self-satisfied anticipation, saying to myself: 'Well, let's get all of these right this time as well.'

The question sheets were distributed, and I looked down at mine. 'What is this? Something's not right here,' I said to myself. Then I could feel the color draining from my face as I realized, in horror, that the questions facing me there on the page were totally different from those that I had previously pictured!

'I've been conned! My guardian spirits have abandoned me!' were the first panicked thoughts that ran through my mind. But fortunately, I didn't have time to luxuriate in such thoughts, as it quickly dawned on me that this was obviously what Heaven had planned for me in direct reaction to my irresponsible lack of serious study. As you can imagine, when I did eventually receive the test results my score was truly miserable.

After this traumatic experience I entered what, for me, was a period of deep self-reflection – the upshot of which was that I found myself humbly apologizing to the gods and my guardian spirits for my poor conduct over those previous few weeks. I remember my words of that time well.

'The first time I did not have enough time to study because I was too busy helping others through my involvement in my university societies, so you were kind enough to provide me with the special spiritual inspiration that allowed me to get those high marks. But there was no reason for me to expect it to happen again. So please forgive me for my conduct,' I said.

So, no matter how much the purpose of our guardian spirits might be to help us, if our requests are of an egotistical nature, or largely motivated by self-interest, carelessness, or laziness, then we cannot expect those guardian spirits to listen to them with favor.

The reason for the lack of response to such requests is that they are heard by high-level spirits residing in the purest heart of the spirit world — and that when they hear wishes of this kind, they begin to worry that the world is going to become filled with lazy people who lack energy and motivation. However, if the petitioner is at the time of the request genuinely doing the very best he can, and if the requests are done adequately and in line with Heaven's will (that is to say, they would really be in the best interests of the individual concerned), then they will allow the person's guardian spirits to provide him with the support he needs.

Sometimes we notice people who, having honed their spiritual sensibilities to a certain degree, then take inordinate pride in their ability to commune with the spirit world or to display their powers of prediction. They would be advised to be extremely cautious in this respect as, although they may be spiritually sensitive, that does not qualify them as exalted individuals in any shape or form. However, if they harness their full potential for the sake of their fellow human beings, and strive to be productive in their everyday lives, then such a person is truly worthy of respect. And in such cases, neither the gods nor their guardian spirits will begrudge their full support.

Gratitude Will Get Your Guardian Spirits Working for You

There is another aspect to our relationship with our guardian spirits that is important, and that is to treat them with the proper courtesy.

In truth, guardian spirits are great sticklers for the rules in this regard; something which probably is a consequence of the fact that the actual lifetimes on Earth of these guardian spirits took place when the feudal system was firmly in place, and rules of propriety were clearly spelled out. It was an era, four or five hundred years ago, when the virtues of filial piety and deference to social superiors was simply taken for granted. Since the guardian spirits were raised in such an age, if you fail to follow the rules of etiquette when dealing with them, then they are certain to be less receptive to your wishes than would otherwise be the case.

Consequently, when you make a request, always make sure that you do so with a proper demeanor and with a mind-set that is fully focused on the task at hand – thus preventing the possibility of false thoughts entering your head at the time you make your appeal. Furthermore, if you should receive a reply to your request, make absolutely sure that you *always* thank your guardian spirits for their help.

It would be best to phrase your thanks something like this:

'Guardian spirits, I thank you deeply for your help. In the future too, I will try to do the best that I can, so please continue to help me in my endeavors.'

Your prayers must at least extend to that. If they do, then your guardian spirits are likely to think:

'Well okay, if he's so grateful for the little we have done for him this time, next time around let's do even more to help.'

In other words, your prayer of thanks will amount to a repeat order for assistance, and will encourage continued efforts from your guardian spirits on your behalf. On the other hand of course, what do you think will happen if you fail to pay your respects to your guardian spirits or to thank them for their past help?

You can almost picture their discontent as they mutter among themselves:

'I can't believe we went all out on this one, and look how the ingrate reacts. Is it too much to expect him to give us a simple word of thanks? Has he got no idea of the meaning of courtesy?'

It is not that guardian spirits are all that desperate for signs of respect, but if they are treated lightly it is natural for them to feel a little out of joint. It is important to remember that, although your guardian spirits are no longer made of flesh and blood, once upon a time they were – and so even though they now inhabit the spiritual world, their emotions remain essentially just like ours. However, because they have become entities with superior spiritual characteristics, they have also come largely to accept the reality of the modern situation, and patiently continue to soldier on, night and day, working for our happiness.

There is a secret method for thanking your guardian spirits, the principle of which I would like to share with you here.

The trick is to frame your words of thanks in the language of the period in which a particular guardian spirit was alive, as languages can change quite radically with the passage of time.

Although the style of language a particular guardian spirit would be accustomed to would vary depending on the age in which he lived, he will forgive any mistakes you might make due to his general appreciation of the trouble you have gone to in trying to communicate in a manner with which he is comfortable.

Of course, since guardian spirits are endowed with powers of telepathy, it doesn't really matter what style of language you use – but if you can match your language to the educational level of the par- ticular guardian spirit, he will certainly appreciate it. It doesn't even matter whether you do a lousy job of it, as long as you are sincere in your approach. This is a typical characteristic of older generations, and it shows how, just as adults will be pleasantly shocked if a child suddenly uses adult speech patterns and expressions, so too will your guardian spirits be moved if you use formal language. If a young child says, 'Father, I am grateful to you from the bottom of my heart,' the bewildered father is likely to think, 'Wow, where on earth could the little fellow have got a mouthful like that from?!' Or say that a son writes his own parents a courtesy letter, in a style more appropriate for dealing with people in formal situations, an old-fashioned father is liable to react with pleasure, thinking, 'Well, well, it seems my boy has finally become a man.' The situation in dealing with your guardian spirits is in many ways comparable.

Regularly thank your guardian spirits in the appropriate style, and you will have the pleasure of finding yourself being rewarded at unexpected times

---

Say you are absolutely exhausted after a hard day's work, but when you get on the subway find that it is jam-packed.

Resigning yourself to a long and uncomfortable ride home standing up, you are surprised to see that the person sitting right in front of you suddenly gets up, allowing you to sit down.

You say to yourself, 'Ah, this looks very much like the work of a guardian spirit! Thank you for your kind help guardian spirit!'

However, sad to say this was actually not an example of the guardian spirits at work. In this case, what really happened was that the person was actually dozing in his seat and had missed his station; then merely jumped up in something of a panic in order to get off at the next station. What can a guardian spirit do at a time like this, when you have given him proper thanks for something which, in actual fact, he was not responsible?

'Okay, Okay. Next time you take the train home I will make sure that I save a seat especially for you,' he then promises.

There is no guardian spirit so hard-hearted as to overlook the thanks proffered by someone he is supposed to be looking after. Instead, he will think, 'This fellow has genuinely made the effort to thank me,' and will think of some way to respond to your thanks in the future. I call this the 'Secret Method for Getting Your Guardian Spirits to Do What You Want.'

BELIEVE IN THESE
WORDS AND YOUR
GOOD FORTUNE
WILL BLOSSOM

POWER CALLS TO MOVE THE DIVINE AND SPIRIT WORLDS

'Kuwabara, Kuwabara'

Whenever I think of the term 'incantation' or 'power call', I immediately think of the phrases 'kuwabara, kuwabara' and 'nanmaidabutsu', which are ancient power calls. Both have an inherent magical existence whose ancient origins do not preclude them from being commonly known in contemporary Japan. 'Kuwabara' started out as a place name. In ancient times, living in the village of this name was a strong-willed girl, who helped a thunder god who had fallen from the clouds to return to the sky. Out of gratitude to the young girl, the god made a promise that lightning would never strike the village. This is the origin of how people came to use the name of that village as an entreaty to the gods.

'Nanmaidabutsu' (pronounced 'nan-my-dabootsu') was derived from the invocation in the name of Amida Bodhisattva, that is 'Namu Amida Butsu', and is derived from the scriptures of the Jodo, or 'Pure Land' sect. I will refrain from going into a detailed explanation here, but suffice to say the basic meaning of the phrase is contained in the idea that the person expressing the incantation turns his or her entire being over to the care

Lucky Fortune

of Amida. In abbreviated form it also sometimes becomes 'Nanmaida' or simply 'Namusan'.

Incantations like 'Kuwabara' or 'Nanmaidabutsu' are easy for the average person to remember – a fundamental requirement of any successful incantation. But on the other hand, if it is too simple, the person using it will not inject their full feeling into it, with the result that it will lose its full effectiveness and fail to bring any significant benefit. So, in this particular case it would be fair to say that simple is not always best.

You may be wondering what the real significance of an incantation or power call is, and why should it be that if we recite an incantation, we are able to drive away evil spirits?

An incantation represents a secret technique which enables us to call down and harness the power of the spirit worlds

---

A power call is like a single ray of sunlight breaking through the clouds – even though those around him will remain trapped in darkness, the person reciting the power call will be bathed in the warmth of bright sunlight.

As for why that should be so, each and every syllable or sound component of the power call has a deep meaning all of its own. This *kotodama* gives off vibrations, with each individual syllable possessing a spiritual vibration in its own right.

And this series of vibrations has the ability to call forth the good fortune power of the gods and spirits.

I would like to introduce next the full list of authentic incantations that originate from the divine and spirit worlds. If you repeat these incantations, then, almost immediately, you will be able to feel the benefit of spiritual power as it wraps itself around and seeps into the internal framework of your body. Basically these are 'incantations to summon help from the spiritual worlds', but in this book I prefer to use a slightly more poetic term, namely 'power calls of the divine and spirit worlds', or 'power calls' for short. However, there is something fundamentally important in their usage that it is essential you remember:

While placing full confidence in the efficacy of the incantations' power, don't rely solely upon them for your success, but also make the greatest possible efforts of your own to secure your wishes

---

I would also like to mention that, when it comes to incantations that have a deeper spiritual resonance, unlike 'Kuwabara' and 'Nanmaidabutsu', they tend to be somewhat difficult to become fully familiar with. But, since fortunately there are not all that many of them, it does become relatively easy to commit them to memory, once you have become comfortable with their pronunciation (see the chart on pages 169 to 170 for instructions on how to remember the power calls easily and use them effectively).

Why Can You Receive Spiritual Power?

When you view the universe from the dimension of the divine and spirit worlds, you can see that the Solar System in which our Earth is located represents a spiritual world all of its own. What actually sets the Earth apart from other bodies in the Solar System is the fact that most of the spirits here are clothed in physical bodies. Moreover, nearly all human beings fail to realize that they have a spiritual dimension that exists within a far greater cosmic whole.

What then, you may wonder, is the nature of the situation for the stars that exist in the boundless universe outside the confines of our own Solar System? Rather than a spiritual existence equivalent to ours, the beings there exist in much higher dimensions – namely the world of the gods or the spirit worlds. It may help if we consider the human beings living on Earth as being run-of-the-mill company employees, then the spirits residing on other planets in our Solar System are section managers or division chiefs, while the gods living in outer space are department chiefs or top executives of a large corporation. The company president, who lives in the outer reaches of space, is the central god known as Sushin.

Normally when we make a request for something, our prayers are heard in the following upward sequential order: human beings (those of the flesh), the spirits, and then the gods. However, a power call is so effective that it has the capacity to cut through the usual chain of command and is heard directly by the divine equivalent of the president or chief executive. In a case where a regular company employee has something bothering him, is the division manager or a member of the board of directors likely to become directly involved? Commonsense tells us that this would probably not be the case. According to the rules governing how a corporation operates, even if a senior executive knew what was bothering a particular company employee, he would more likely call the person's immediate superior, the section chief or division chief, and let him know about it. He would say something like this:

'Sorry, but it has come to my attention that Mr X has something on his mind. He's asked me to help, so would you mind seeing what he's upset about.'

The division chief would then quickly arrange a meeting with the employee in question, and together they would try to find a solution to the problem. The actions of the 'division chief' are, from beginning to end, supervised by the divine spirits from their Takamikura palace in the divine world. They assign the section chief to handle the whole problem with the employee, and entrust him with the power to follow it through, in what is a typical example of finely-tuned 'spiritual service'.

But to believe that by simply relying on power calls you can expect to receive this quality of service would be wishful thinking. However, this kind of invaluable good fortune can genuinely become yours through a combination of the use of these amazing power calls and a steadfast belief in your own abilities. These calls hold the potential to cause your luck to make explosive leaps forward — even 100-fold improvements are not unheard of. With them you have the tools at your disposal to make your life brighter, and see your happiness improve dozens of times over.

THE FIRST POWER CALL

Intone and Good Spirits Will Gather

The first one of these extraordinary power calls that I want to introduce you to is:

SENTEN NAMU FURUHOBIRU

What on earth is that, many of you are probably saying to your-selves in puzzlement right now. And such a reaction is certainly understandable – after all, this is an expression that you have probably never heard before. However, let me assure you that this power call, more than any other I'm going to discuss, has the capability to cause a radical transformation within your spiritual universe.

The actual process whereby spiritual power descends to Earth is as follows:

- ✳ the individual intones a power call,
- ✳ this is heard in the divine world,
- ✳ it is then passed on down to the spirit world,
- ✳ which, in turn, responds to the appeal from the individual.

The response from the divine spirit world will differ depending on the type of power call employed. This particular power call, SENTEN NAMU FURUHOBIRU (pronounced 'sen-ten namu furu-hobiroo'), is referred to as a 'faith incantation', because central

to its efficacy is the principle that faith binds everything together in a mutually dependent relationship.

At this point it is important to recognize that if

you only half believe in the efficacy of these power calls, they will have no effect whatsoever. But if you can muster the strength of faith to overcome any doubts, then you will be able to receive a wealth of spiritual benefits.

First of all, the primal energy or *ki* of good spirits (beginning with that of your guardian spirits, along with the more general forces of good fortune), will combine and act as a great protective force for your lasting welfare. Secondly, you and your guardian spirits will come together in a sense of spiritual union and mutual awareness, thus greatly sharpening your spiritual senses.

This double effect serves to keep away disasters, and invite the benefits of positive destiny. At the same time you will discover corresponding gains in the way your lifestyle becomes more forward-oriented, your mind and body feel rejuvenated with the vigor of good health, and you find yourself easily able to dispel the dark clouds of sadness and depression. Yet another notable advantage that may be of help to some, is the ability to invigorate the spiritual energy of both animals and plants through the use of this all-encompassing power call.

The '2:8 Noodles' Principle

There is a technique for making noodles in my home country of Japan known as *nihachi soba*, which literally means '2:8 noodles'. This comes from the proportions used to make the noodles – which traditionally comprise eight parts soba powder to two parts water, and are said to guarantee the most delicious soba noodles possible. Why did I suddenly bring up the topic of soba noodles? Because this 2:8 proportion of ingredients closely parallels the proportions required in the relationship between power calls and faith.

You need to possess eight parts' faith before you can place trust in the power call to make up the two remaining parts of your commitment

---

If you can achieve these proportions, then you will enjoy overwhelming support from a divine world that recognizes the extent of your faith and rewards you accordingly.

Most important of all is for you to feel confident in your faith and to forcefully express it in the following statements:

'I am becoming stronger and stronger through the power calls, and am receiving the protection I need. The direction my fate is taking is improving enormously.'

This might be said to be the *nihachi soba* principle at work. Since this principle applies to all the power calls, and not just to SENTEN NAMU FURUHOBIRU, I feel that I cannot overemphasize the importance of remembering it.

Even if you fully memorize and intone the power calls, your words alone will not be enough to attract the attention of Heaven – you must supplement them with all the sincerity you can possibly muster, and have absolute faith that they will have the intended effects. That sincerity will, in effect, be transformed into a spiritual energy with the ability to influence Heaven. If you think of the power   calls as letters that are sent to the divine and spirit worlds, then your sincerity and faith are the stamps that ensure they are delivered. If you fail to affix the required stamps then the letters are unlikely to reach their intended destination.

Assuming that you do affix the correct postage to your letters – that is to say, you perform the power call with the correct attitude – then instantly the spiritual mailman will show up to take your letters to the divine and spirit worlds. Here your letter will be carefully read to ensure it is not selfishly motivated, that what you are asking for will not cause unhappiness to others, and that it contains no other aspects of which the spirits may disapprove. If what you ask for is considered by the divine spirits to be for the general benefit of the world and humanity, then a reply will quickly be sent to you via the guardian spirits. On occasion, however, the reply will go directly from the divine spirit world to the person making the appeal.

Grow Into a Person
Resembling a Giant Tree

A bonsai tree in its pot is great to look at, but that is the only purpose it serves. On the other hand a large tree, with its roots running strong and deep through the earth, besides being an object of distinguished splendor, offers a place of rest for humans and animals alike. And even if such a tree is felled, its timber can still be used in a positive way to help build a home or a bridge. Although both are 'trees', they are two very different kinds of tree. Similarly, we might talk of people that resemble 'planted bonsai trees' or 'giant naturally growing trees'.

So a great sense of mission, allied to strong willpower, might be compared to the trunk of a great tree, while action is comparable to the limbs and branches that sprout from it. The results of this combined purpose and action are the rich 'fruits' that appear littered among the leaves. In order for us to enjoy a 'highly fruitful life' it makes sense that we should attempt to follow this pattern, which requires us to have a healthy system of roots and branches.

If we only have one life to live, then we should retain an attitude that encourages us to become a great tree – something capable of providing support and help to a great many people

---

You should be thinking something along these lines:

'Dear guardian spirit, thank you for your constant protection. Please give me guidance so that I may become strong, wise, sturdy, and able to bring happiness to others.'

If you can develop the habit of thinking like this from an early age, you have a very good chance of becoming a person who enjoys extraordinarily good luck. Through the use of the power calls you will be able to build a strong spiritual base, and from this base it will be possible for a bountiful crop of rich, tasty fruit to develop. In fact, rather than being merely possible, it will be inevitable. So when intoning **SENTEN NAMU FURUHOBIRU**, have faith that you will become a person whose belief and power stretch skyward like the branches of a great tree.

It's Incredible! Bullying is Caused by Mischievous Spirits

One of the beneficial effects that the use of power calls brings to us is the ability to avoid one of the most worrying social problems that plague many young people: the problem of bullying. But before explaining the method involved, we need to analyze the bullying phenomenon from the spiritual perspective. I can cite the following as root causes:

1. The problem is caused by spiteful spirits intent on reaping vengeance upon successive generations of your family.
2. The problem is caused by the jealous and/or envious spirit of an aborted child, who holds his brother, sister, or parents responsible for the decision that deprived him of a life on earth.
3. The mischievous spirits of baby racoons or foxes are haunting either the school and/or its immediate surroundings.
4. The children who are actually committing the bullying have seen too many violent movies and TV, and have developed a subconscious tendency to engage in such conduct themselves.

When a child is being bullied by his peers, his or her attitude will start to show tell-tale signs of negativity and depression. The individual is probably not even aware of this development himself, but such a situation has the unfortunate effect of quickly attracting the attention of mischievous and spiteful spirits. Pretty soon the child's classmates end up feeling 'There's something about that guy that I just can't stand' – with the end result that, no matter how bright and cheerful the child tries to be, evil spirits will maintain a menacing presence around him, and his classmates will eventually feel compelled to pick on him.

Usually the children who are doing the bullying are also at the same time unconsciously under the controlling influence of evil spirits. Before they know it these children are thinking, 'I don't know why, but I hate such pathetic kids,' or, 'I don't know why, but I can't help picking on other kids.'

But no matter how dreadful a person's behavior might be, he always has a conscience hidden inside. Even bullies who hit, kick, or knock other kids down, will tell you that, deep down, they really don't want to act that way. The reason why they continue with such intimidation, even though deep inside they want to stop, can be apportioned to the fact that they are being directed in their actions by evil spirits.

What we might call a 'persecuting spirit' has actually taken control of the hearts of these children. Therefore, the real enemy, both of the bullies as well as those unfortunate ones being picked on, are these 'persecuting spirits'.

Bullying Spirits Form Gangs

Spirits that cause children to intimidate others are usually weak in character. In many cases, these spirits are incapable of doing anything on their own, but once formed into gangs can exert a very considerable influence over the people they choose to plague.

Especially at school, we often find such groups are made up of the spirits of little *tanuki* racoon dogs or little foxes. These animal spirits gather into large groups and then, as their own sick form of entertainment, choose some weak child to bully — finding nothing more pleasing than to see a child so intimidated that they break down into tears.

When groups of children get together to bully the two or three victims that they have chosen, it is purely because the evil spirits have formed a gang that has the collective power to heavily influence them in their actions. But spirits are only able to exert this collective power because people allow them to do so. If someone wakes up thinking: 'Chances are I'll probably pick on someone today,' or 'I'm going to really sort out that pathetic creep when I see him at school this afternoon,' it performs the function of encouraging the evil spirits in their attempts to per-suade the child to translate those intentions into actual action later in the day.

If a child, understandably, finds himself thinking, 'I'm scared, I'm really scared,' when faced with a group of bullies, then a 'persecuting spirit' will immediately recognize that feeling and say to his cohorts, 'Hey, look. The kid's so scared of us he might mess his shorts. Let's really go to town on him this time.' It's sad but, in effect, feelings of fear actually encourage 'bullying spirits' to redouble their efforts.

Kids doing the bullying will often find themselves dreaming up further bad things to do to their victims. 'Today we could steal the kid's lunch money,' or 'Let's break all his pens,' are typical ideas they may be hatching – with the end result that as they visualize these scenes, they are unaware that such a process serves to further attract the attentions of these evil spirits.

The more established and regular these ideas among the bullies and their victims become, the larger in number and stronger in influence the evil spirits will grow. Sadly, in the end, both sides of this ugly relationship ultimately end up being victims of the evil spirits, who revel in such poisonous conditions.

How to Get Rid of Mischievous Spirits

In order to protect yourself from intimidating spirits, you should attempt to do the following three things:

① Have confidence. Discover something that you can excel at, be it within the realm of study, sports, or whatever. Develop and take pride in this strong point you have found.

② Become physically strong. If you are a little short of height, or your legs are quite short, there is nothing you can do about it as they are usually features inherited from your parents. But you can improve your bodily strength. If you can keep your stomach in good shape and develop something of an iron constitution, your own spirit will become stronger, as will the spirits who give you their support. It is certainly not to your advantage to be a weak and sickly person.

3 Develop greater determination and willpower to see things right through to the end. Even if you see everyone else around you falling by the wayside, don't give up until you achieve your goal! Such a strong sense of determination will fortify your personal aura and make it much more of a daunting proposition for evil spirits to approach you.

If you follow these three rules, no 'intimidating spirits' will be able to get close to you – although, of course, it goes without saying that one major premise here is that you will all the while be using the power call **SENTEN NAMU FURUHOBIRU**.

But why is it that by sticking to these three rules you can send the 'bullying spirits' into retreat? The answer (once again) lies in how things appear from the perspective of the spirit world.

Firstly, when it comes to point 1 (and as I explained earlier), the 'bullying spirits' are pretty spineless when they are on their own.

But when they get together in groups they gain in confidence, even though their basic character remains essentially the same. So if you engage in a process that promotes greater self-confidence, as part of that process you should say to yourself,

'Even if I'm not much good when it comes to study, when it comes to sport I'm not about to lose to anybody!'

This will create an aura of strength around you, something which will grow even more formidable when your guardian spirits join in their support, and which will in turn leave the evil spirits broken and defeated.

Next, when it comes to point 2, individuals who have difficulty in getting out of bed in the morning, or who regularly suffer from nightmares, are frequently people with weak constitutions. These kinds of people, who suffer from what is referred to as a 'weak spiritual character', often become the target of evil spirits. Therefore it is recommended that in order to combat this weakness, you try to develop a healthy body, which allows you to comfortably eat all kinds of food. Since all food contains spiritual essence, when you eat you should remind yourself how the nourishment from that spiritual essence will help to keep you well. Furthermore, if you increase your body strength, you will then be able to tackle your studies, sport, or other pursuits with much greater energy, focus, and attendant success.

The old expression goes, 'A sound mind in a sound body,' but in this case it might be slightly more appropriate to say, 'A sound spirit in a sound body' – as an added benefit of improving your physical condition, the aura and spiritual energy that extends throughout your body becomes considerably stronger. This gives the advantage of forcing the evil spirits to keep their distance, or simply to look elsewhere for their sinister entertainment.

Finally, we have point 3 – 'Hang in there! Don't be beaten!' If you can always maintain this kind of attitude, the strength of your conviction and your sense of determination will increase enormously.

Nen-riki or 'the power of thought' is key in keeping the forces of evil at bay

---

However, if this power of thought is of the wrong kind, then it will perform the function of attracting evil spirits. But if there is a positive usage of the power of thought, and you say to yourself,

'I'm not going to let myself be controlled by any intimidating spirit,'

or

'Since my guardian spirit is always watching over me, I'm certain to be okay.'

you will find the evil spirits' approaches ineffective. Since these good thoughts serve to attract large numbers of friendly spirits, evil spirits find themselves largely impotent in their attempts to exercise influence over your destiny, and are unable to put up any resistance against the overwhelming strength of your protective spirits.

If you follow the methods I have outlined above, you should have absolutely no problem in avoiding the poisonous attentions of evil spirits.

How to Attract and Use an Army of Guardian Spirits to the Full

Here I would like to explain the most effective method for making use of the power call SENTEN NAMU FURUHOBIRU.

Imagine a picture of several different human faces, collectively forming a single larger human face. If you stare for a period of time at such a picture, you will slowly but surely begin to feel a sense of power rising from the core of your conscious being. When you chant the power call **SENTEN NAMU FURUHOBIRU**, what actually happens is that an army of guardian spirits gathers around you and collectively takes on an appearance very similar in style to this picture.

It is recommended that you give this power call in a quiet room, detached from the bustle of family or work, and at a time when you are feeling calm and relaxed. Then, on a suitable piece of paper try to sketch this army of guardian spirits as a picture of them forms in your own mind. In the vision you see, you will notice that the faces are bright and shiny, and are all laughing loudly. At this point there is no need to concentrate on anything too difficult – simply try to put down on paper the image that you have formed in your head.

After you have drawn a collective portrait of this power group – which, in effect, is the powerful guardian spirit army watching over you – attach it somewhere in your room that is immediately visible. This is in order that when you are invoking the power call, you can always look at this picture and think to yourself:

'The combined power of all these united forces is now lodged within me. I will not be beaten!'

If you follow this procedure, you will gain the benefit of acquiring a true and profound power that extends throughout the entire fabric of your physical and spiritual being. (Note: If you use the power call in conjunction with the *divine world logo* shown in Chapter 5, it will serve to further increase its effectiveness.) Furthermore, if you believe that you suffer from certain personal weaknesses, discipline yourself to think in such a way as to eliminate the defects in question. For example, if you think that perhaps you lack a sense of perseverance, say to yourself:

'In reality I have plenty of perseverance. There's absolutely no reason why I shouldn't be able to tough it out with the best of them.'

Or if someone chooses to call you a 'weakling' or 'coward', reaffirm to yourself out loud:

'I'm not a weakling, or a coward. I'm filled with the courage of my own worth and have the united power of my guardian spirits to support me.'

Say it and believe it. The fact is that by using this power call you will make great gains in both the strength of your inner conviction and in the levels of your own personal confidence.

Faith creates power

As I explained before when discussing the '2:8 noodle principle', if you have security in your faith, the power that this provides will supplement your own inherent capabilities, and will encourage a formidable army of benevolent guardian spirits to gather around you. You should get a notebook and write down:

'I have courage. My guardian spirits are looking out for me.'

Then say the same thing out loud, and continuously picture yourself as being both strong and confident. If you fulfill this series of acts, then your faith will continue to deepen.

Remember that your cadre of guardian spirits is always by your side. Have faith in that truth. This is collectively what is known as the 'Secret Method for Prompting your Army of Guardian Spirits into Action'.

Evil Spirits Also Attack in Armies

If you can employ this 'secret method', you will immediately find that deep within the central core of your consciousness, there is a welling-up sensation of strength and inner confidence. But again you must always remember to thank the divine world and your guardian spirits for their assistance, and not brag to your friends and family of the method you have used. If you do fail to give thanks, then evil spirits will quickly attach themselves to you with the consequence that the power you previously enjoyed will be immediately negated. And if you do find that your power source has been shut down, this will have the knock-on effect of damaging your self-confidence, and leaving you prone to an obsession with negative thoughts and fears of failure. Viewing the situation from the standpoint of the spirit world, what is happening in such

a case is that your army of guardian spirits is being separated and scattered, and the unique power that they possessed when in unity is now being dissipated.

On top of all this, what then happens is that the evil spirits band together to form an army of their own, and gradually expand their strength as their ranks are swelled by the recruitment of other evil spirits happy to join in the pursuit of wickedness. As your army of guardian spirits is driven away in disarray, this army of evil spirits will quickly approach you, and you will begin to find yourself in what amounts to a situation fraught with danger: something like a rudderless spaceship being dragged helplessly into the sad, empty desolation of a black hole.

There is, however, a method to escape falling into this dark oblivion seething with the contorted torment of evil spirits: regularly reassure yourself that your army of guardian spirits will ultimately be victorious, and constantly reflect upon what recent actions and thoughts of yours may have been unworthy or selfish. There is always a reason why your power has stopped flowing, and you need to carefully consider what that reason might be. And if you realize that there is indeed some point on which you need to carefully reflect (the most common of which are, incidentally, 'pride' and 'spiritual laziness'), then you should do so with a sense of total honesty and sincerity. With the completion of this process spiritual power will once again be able to make its clear, uninterrupted flow down from the spirit world, and allow for the formation of a new army of powerful guardian spirits.

If conditions in the present material world are viewed from the standpoint of the divine and spirit worlds, it can be seen that deceiving spirits, evil spirits, and other poisonous or corrupted spirits of various kinds are both numerous and very much present in our world. This is especially true because developments in modern society mean that people no longer tend to invest proper respect in traditional figures of authority or older members of the community, and, as a consequence, there is an attendant lack of moral and ethical education in schools, the family, and society at large.

Children no longer understand whom they should respect or how to go about doing it, and as a result tend to do just as they please. And since most adults these days also tend to have a self-serving attitude that says 'As long as I'm okay, I don't care what happens to anyone else,' such thinking can't help but be reflected in attitudes within the spirit world. However, because in most cases guardian spirits were originally individuals who lived in an earlier age of our planet's history, they are inclined to stick to more traditional forms of courtesy and decorum, and to strongly observe principles based on honor and respect. So, if you treat them in a fashion which acknowledges these time-honored preferences, then they will be far more willing to serve as your allies.

Because evil spirits are opportunistic, they can quickly form into groups and attack people who are unaware of their proximity and are unprepared for their assault. As noted earlier, what evil spirits do not like are people who are self-confident, physically strong, and who observe honest and decent thinking – so if you use spiritual power to strengthen yourself in these key areas, while at the same time invoking the appropriate power calls, you can be assured that an army of guardian spirits will determinedly protect you from the cruel attacks of these evil spirits. In days gone by, tools such as garlic, crucifixes or rosaries were traditionally used to ward off evil spirits (especially in the West), but now we are in an age when power calls and faith provide a more comprehensive and secure protection from their sinister attentions.

THE SECOND POWER CALL

The Power Symbolized by Fudo Myoo

Usually 'bullying spirits' will be driven away by the protective shield resulting from your unification with your guardian spirits through the use of the power call SENTEN NAMU FURUHOBIRU. But there may be other occasions when you might be unfortunate enough to encounter groups of 'bullying spirits' who are in possession of potent powers capable of overpowering these precautionary measures. In such an event, it is best to call Fudo Myoo to your assistance.

The second major incantation in the power call rankings is the one used to call forth the help of Fudo Myoo (Acala) – the God of Fire. It is an SOS signal to get this heavenly king to start acting on your behalf.

The call is as follows:

NOHMAKUSAHMANDA BAHZARADANSENDA MAKAROSHADA SOWATAYA UNTARA TAKANMAN

'Slow down!' you are probably saying to yourself. 'What an incredibly long power call, I'll never be able to remember that.' Thankfully, however, there is an abbreviated, and much easier version. Just say: **NOHMAKUSAHMANDA BAZARADANKAN** (which can be pronounced as 'no-maqusa-manda ba-zara-dan-can'). Since many of you won't have an accurate idea of who the deity Fudo Myoo is, I would like to take this chance to give you a little background information. Simply put, Fudo Myoo is one of the guardian spirits in the Buddhist pantheon of deities. He is usually said to be a descendant of Dainichi Nyorai (Mahāvairocana-satathāgata), but is actually a descendant of Kunitokotachi no Mikoto, an ancestral God of the Earth. Fudo Myoo expresses in his actions 'an unwavering belief in the refusal to forgive evil', and possesses the power required to suppress evil spirits and other threats of menace. This deity is usually depicted in paintings as a

fearsome character surrounded by billowing clouds of fire, with, in his right hand, the sword of resolution (a magic sword able to subdue and exorcise evil spirits), and in his left hand a rope that represents the power of the *dharma*, or law (although it can also be considered to represent self-sufficiency).

Although initially daunting in appearance he is actually a kind and trustworthy guardian spirit, whose only desire is to bring under control any villain that he may encounter. It is of further comfort to know that when Fudo Myoo becomes directly involved in your struggles, the power wielded by your unified band of guardian spirits actually increases by a factor of three.

In order to make sure that you are taking full advantage of the power of King Fudo Myoo, you should draw an image of him on a piece of paper and then employ the power call while gazing intently at it. Place the image of the face of Fudo Myoo – the symbol of immovable faith – in the center of the piece of paper, and then sketch the faces of the band of guardian spirits around it, so that you finally end up with a collection of drawn faces. Remember, it is wise to make the faces of the guardian spirits resemble those of your own parents and grandparents, which, genetics dictate, will be close to those of your real guardian spirits.

In this case too, it is truly important to remain strong in your faith. After all, Fudo Myoo is the symbol of unwavering faith.

In order to take full advantage of his power, it is useless to give the power call in a half-hearted manner, saying, 'I guess this will probably do' or some similar wishy-washy phrase

---

You must say to yourself, 'No doubt about it, things are sure to turn out okay!' while giving a full-blooded power call aimed at enlisting the formidable aid of Fudo Myoo.

By paying heed to the various points I have given in my explanation above, you will be able to attack and ultimately drive away any band of 'bullying spirits'. As for those who are likely to be either the victim of bullying, or the actual bullies themselves, you should seek to avoid being controlled by evil spirits through a greater belief in the existence of guardian spirits who are ready and willing to help. This positive belief will enable you to live your life in a positive manner, confident in the knowledge that you possess the strength of spirit to reject the influences of evil. I have found that the benefits of such an attitude adjustment are particularly apparent for strong-willed company employees, and those generally sensitive to the presence of spirits.

THE THIRD POWER CALL

The Effectiveness of Praying to the North Star

Now let me introduce you to the third of the 'Big Three' power calls:

UNTEN TOHBOH EHTAHTO

This power call (pronounced 'un-ten toh-boh e-ta-toh') will

directly reach the god of the North Star, and a direct answer will correspondingly come back to the person who has invoked it. There is an old Japanese saying, 'When disaster goes out the window, good fortune comes rushing in,' which conveys a little of what this power call means. It can be considered to be at its most effective when you are feeling down in the dumps, but that is not the only time when it can be used to drive away the dark clouds of misfortune. It is also perfect for times when you have suffered from bad dreams, on days when your horoscope is poor, when one's biorhythms are out of sync, or on any other number of similar occasions when things aren't quite working out as you'd hoped.

The North Star is home to a deity by the name of Tyros (who is also known as 'Old Man Taiotsu'), and all the wisdom of the universe is lodged within the omniscient mind of this god. At the same time, this great god is privy to all the myriad secrets of hereditary fate – which makes it good sense to pray to him for all kinds of things, such as safety while driving, success in school, or even the successful expansion of your business.

There is the expression 'Everything is known to the stars.' And with the profound existence of the god Tyros such a saying can be considered perfectly accurate – for he has an all-encompassing knowledge of the past, and the future, and even what lies hidden within the deepest recesses of men's hearts. For this reason, if when you pray it is with a devout honesty and sincerity, he is certain to recognize the genuine sentiment of your words and answer your prayers directly.

The god Tyros possesses ultimate responsibility over the entire realm of the divine worlds, and as part of his existence exercises his great power to control the guardian spirits, the gods living in the other stars, and all the celestial bodies besides. Worshipped by the ancient Chinese as Tiandi or the 'Heavenly King', the scope and grandeur of his powers means that it would probably be most fitting to refer to him as the 'Supreme God'.

For untold ages, the North Star has stood in the same spot in the night sky, acting as a constant, immovable point of reference on which mankind has established all of its standards: travellers have constantly checked from which direction the North Star is shining as they chart their journey; in ancient times massive structures were constructed in alignment with its position; and it serves as the axis around which the seasonal constellations revolve. Its deep significance is such that it is almost as if this eternal star were continuously watching over us. During the daytime the light from the sun is so bright that the North Star remains invisible to the naked eye, but it still hangs there as an eternal beacon to guide mankind in the direction of true north.

There are a myriad of stars shining in the night sky – but it remains easy to pick out the North Star from among them. So once you have picked out the brightly sparkling North Star as it sits in the direction of true north, direct the following power call to the god Tyros who resides there: UNTEN TOHBOH EHTAHTO. If you don't have any specific request to make at that time, simply make sure that you imbue your power call with a feeling of gratitude. A simple prayer like 'Please protect me from disease and keep my family safe from harm' will probably prove more effective than any magical incantation.

Santa Claus is the North Star Deity

The popular legend is that Santa Claus visits us on Christmas Eve – but in reality Santa Claus is nothing more than a motif representing Tyros of the North Star.

I know that quite a few of my readers will have serious doubts about this statement. But those of us endowed with the powers of spiritual insight know that Santa Claus and Tyros look exactly alike, and that in reality it is Tyros who comes visiting us at Christmas from his home in the North Star. Of course, what I mean when I say this is that Santa Claus is really a subsidiary manifestation of Tyros, who personally only visits our planet once every 50 years.

According to the generally accepted version of the Santa Claus legend, he was a saint of early Christianity who gave presents to impoverished children. Over time that simple story developed into the legend we know today of a jolly old fellow with a red outfit and white beard, who rides through the sky on a sleigh drawn by his team of reindeer.

It is the kind of story guaranteed to delight any child. But this is in actual fact exactly the appearance Tyros takes on when he visits Earth – he has a white beard and is carried across the sky by flying reindeer. No doubt there are people who believe that myths and fairytales are simply fabricated stories and therefore of no real value. But such a cynical attitude is something of a shame and deprives people of a knowledge which extends beyond the purely rational. Usually people with a strong psychic sense have the ability to perceive the truth, and they are the ones who tell or write down such stories, thereby unconsciously fashioning them into the stories that eventually pass into the realms of myth and legend.

The enduring image for most of us is of Santa Claus sitting in a reindeer-drawn sleigh, with a sack behind him packed with presents to deliver to the world's children. White beard, white hair … no that's not right! The hair is the problem. Although Santa is supposed to be wearing a red cap, beneath it he is completely bald. That's right. Santa Claus – in fact the deity Tyros – actually resembles a bald-headed old fellow. If you happen to see Santa Claus in a dream, try asking him about it. Say: 'Go on, please take off your cap.' No doubt such a request will cause him to look a little bashful, but he will still probably go ahead and show you his shiny pate. And because he is a very kindly deity, he won't get angry or make any nasty comments about the quality of your ancestry. So don't worry, just go ahead and ask.

Folklore tells us that Santa Claus puts presents into our Christmas stockings, and Tyros does exactly the same – except for one fundamental respect: what he will put in your stocking is not the toys or sweets that you were expecting, but the following words of encouragement:

'Pin down the course of your life, and while remaining
careful, have the faith to step forward with confidence'

This is the overwhelming desire of the god Tyros, which is cap-tured within the gift of advice he gives you. But don't whimper and complain by saying, 'What's this? Where are

my *presents*?' because even the divine and spirit worlds will become thoroughly disgusted if you constantly keep throwing the power call UNTEN TOHBOH EHTAHTO in their direction in a one-sided fashion – without appreciating the immeasurable value that such advice represents.

However, if instead you offer a prayer like the following, the god Tyros will be overjoyed:

'I understand fully what the divine and spiritual worlds want of me. And since I am really trying to become the kind of person who will do my best to comply with your wishes, please lend me the strength to see it through. UNTEN TOHBOH EHTAHTO.'

He might then reply as follows:

'Is that so? Well then, let's reduce the bad karma from your previous lives which has been holding you back, and increase the levels of your good fortune a hundred times over.'

An understanding of the guiding principles governing the relationship between Tyros and yourself is the key to deepening your interaction with the divine and spirit worlds. It is not exactly a matter of give and take – but it is important that each side knows what the other one desires, and that over the long haul both try their hardest to achieve success together.

If you have read this far, it means you will appreciate this message I now pass on from Tyros:

'Study hard, and work to become the kind of person who will be of use to others and a benefit to society in general'

This is really a special present. You might say that it represents the collective wish of the divine and spirit worlds.

Incidentally, the best time to direct your prayers to the North Star is around the 15th of each month, as this date corresponds to the beginning of the month according to the old lunar calendar. If you pray at this time, you are likely to find more of your wishes being fulfilled.

Use the Power Calls to Get on Good Terms with the Divine and Spirit Worlds

The highest dimensions of the divine and spirit worlds exist in places so staggeringly distant that they almost defy the imagination. Far beyond just a few thousand or tens of thousands of light years from Earth, they exist millions upon millions of light years beyond the Milky Way, the Andromeda Nebula and other more commonly known constellations. In three-dimensional terms, the time required to cover such vast distances is mind boggling, and simply impossible for a human being to cover, encumbered as we are by the constraints of our physical bodies. However, if one enters the fourth and fifth dimensions, or even beyond those into the sixth and seventh dimensions, then time and space become irrelevant, and we are free to go wherever in the universe we please.

Since Tyros and the other deities exist in the higher dimensions, although we say they reside in the incredibly distant North

Star, Andromeda Nebula, or wherever, they can still visit the Earth any time they please. However, they never choose to simply wander down to Earth without good reason: their visits are prompted only by a clearly defined purpose.

So in the event that they do have some function to perform on Earth, then naturally enough they arrive at a location consistent with the demands of that assignment. We can employ a power call to say, 'Come here please,' but in all circumstances this amounts to nothing more than an optimistic request, and should always be delivered both with the head bowed and with a due sense of respect.

As I pointed out earlier, we want to try to get the divine spirits to say to themselves: 'I want to go see what he's up to.' The idea being to anticipate the desires of the divine and spirit worlds and thereby transform them into reality. This is an approach which, without doubt, represents the most effective method for handling these kind of situations.

The central aim remains to live a life in which your attitude and your clearly defined goals will cause the divine spirits to gather around you without you having to make any kind of conscious effort. If someone resolutely strives for the benefit of mankind and for the planet (on which we all depend for survival), then they can feel secure in looking forward to the divine and spirit worlds coming together in unified support of their actions.

By now this discussion has become a little bit complex, but I firmly believe that if you can learn to understand exactly how the divine world operates — that is to say the processes and rules involved — then you will come to have a greater belief in the efficacy of the power calls.

The fact is that Tyros and the other gods would ideally like to enjoy a friendly relationship with all of us here on Earth, but as we human beings increasingly find ourselves acting in a more materialist and selfish manner, we find the spiritual aspect of our existence becoming closed to such a degree that we can no longer hear the voices of the gods.

The key to this deteriorating situation is to open your heart.

Reawaken your friendship with the gods

If you can do this, you will soon witness great improvements in the direction your fortunes are taking, and a lasting happiness you previously thought lay well beyond your grasp.

THE FOURTH POWER CALL

Break the Chains with North Star Power

Let me introduce you to another power call: one that is particularly effective in breaking free from spiritual chains, and which also has the North Star as its origin:

HONBORA SOMOBIRU FURUFURUFURU

This one is quite easy to remember, and has the added advantage that anyone can enjoy the benefits it brings after using it only once or twice. I strongly recommend that you immediately start putting this power call to use as a ready technique to drive away the malicious spirits that you may feel have recently been holding you back in your attempts at success.

The technique to employ with this particular power call is remarkably simple. Just keep repeating HONBORA SOMOBIRU FURUFURU-FURU, or 'hon-bora somo-biroo fu-roo-fu-roo-fu-roo'. It is best to repeat the call about 36 times, although there is really no need to worry too much about the exact number of repetitions, and it is preferable while doing so to picture in your

Believe in These Words and Your Good Fortune Will Blossom

127

mind the images of the North Star shining in the night sky and the god Tyros who lives there.

If you could actually view things in the spiritual dimensions, you would see that the words that emerge from your mouth – referred to as *kotodama* – take on the form of an essence, which

possesses innate power to drive away evil spirits. As the essence disperses from your mouth it performs the function of uniting you with your guardian spirits. It also has the capability, when required, to drive away the malicious spirits that tend to gather around us.

'Hey there! You little devils. Stop hanging around here. You're not going to make any kind of progress with this person as long as we're around to protect him. Get out of here!'

Your army of guardian spirits may say this to the mischievous attackers, as they quickly surround you in response to the evocation of this power call.

A typical reaction to such a rejection would be for the little devils to cringe down in abject fear and weakly plead, 'We're so sorry. Please forgive us this time,' as they quickly took in the reality of the situation and realized they were hopelessly outgunned.

Faced with such overpowering odds, this army of evil spirits,

who wickedly choose to torment people by drag-
ging them back with the use of their invisible spiritual chains, will then take to their heels in a
frenzied retreat of fright and confusion. In the

fastest of cases that use this power call, the constraining chains
will drop away in a matter of only a few seconds, although, as
with the use of the other power calls we have mentioned, a fundamental lack of faith in their abilities will sadly render usage of
the calls largely ineffectual.

The little devils will probably react to the presence of such
doubts by saying something like:

'Well, guardian spirits, this guy obviously still doubts whether
what you say will really work. It would seem he has more
belief in us, the ones responsible for tying him down and
holding him back from the success that was due to him, than
you. Guardian spirits, we understand your noble desire to
help, but it seems pretty obvious that we have the upper
hand in this particular battle. Perhaps you'd best leave the
fellow to our tender mercies.'

During this spiritual battle of wills, the person in question will be
left to suffer in a cold sweat; haunted by a dim, subconscious
awareness of the precarious balance in which his fate hangs.

Since this is the case, when you use this **HONBORA SOMO-
BIRU FURUFURUFURU** power call, make sure that inside your

heart you are also saying, with all the spiritual willpower at your command,

'I have absolutely no doubt those evil little devils will be unsuccessful in their wicked schemes.'

For if you repeat it only half-heartedly, you could be exposing yourself to the very serious danger of becoming hopelessly swamped by these evil creatures.

Star Wars – A Metaphor for North Star Power

The hugely popular *Star Wars* movie trilogy has direct relevance to North Star power. Its principal hero, Luke Skywalker, relies on his faith in the 'Force' to overcome Darth Vader, the embodiment of evil. In the early stages of the story Luke has his doubts about the very existence of the 'Force', and as the films progress the overcoming of these doubts create a plotline whereby his 'conviction' becomes a method for polishing or refining this faith. However, Darth Vader, as a former noble 'Jedi', also has the ability to harness the power of the 'Force', and the finely balanced conflict between these two opposing forces becomes the central theme that dictates the rest of the action.

The climax of the series comes with the duel between Luke

Skywalker and Darth Vader: the meeting between two warriors endowed with incredibly strong, but diametrically opposed faiths, upon which the fate of mankind depends.

Another intriguing aspect of the films is how, although the Evil Empire possesses within its armouries huge amounts of firepower and the technologies to enable it to destroy whole plan-

ets, in the final battle it is the power of faith that eventually wins out.

When his aged mentor, Obi-Wan Kenobi, is teaching Luke how to fight and tells him, 'Luke, trust the Force.' Luke, who is more at home with modern weapons, finds his advice ludicrous, saying, 'What? You mean THAT!'

So Luke found himself in the exact same position as those of us living today. Our immediate reaction is to say, 'What? How could there possibly be any kind of "power" coming from the divine and spirit worlds?'

Living as we do in a scientific age when men have sent rockets to the moon and planes can fly us anywhere in the world within 24 hours, it may seem strange to talk about things like faith and divine power when faced everywhere by man's ability to over-come the physical. Looking at things from an entirely scientific perspective that may be true, but life's experiences teach us that people still have a lot of undeveloped capabilities hidden within them.

> It is at those times when we believe in the possibility of phenomena beyond the purely rational that we are presented with the chance to enhance our innate capabilities

Since ancient times it has been proposed that our world is simply a manifestation of the divine and spiritual worlds, and stories such as *Star Wars* ably demonstrate how the power of the North Star divine world is accurately translated into stories which help to shape our lives in this one.

Tyros, the deity of the North Star, is always trying to communicate his message to us, just as Obi-Wan Kenobi did with Luke Skywalker. He is telling us:

'Have faith in the power of the North Star. Believe in the power of the worlds of the gods and spirits.'

If you can accept his encouragement, and employ the power calls with a sense of genuine faith and conviction, then you too can become a person of purity and goodness, like Luke Skywalker – while at the same time you will begin to enjoy the rewards of a radical upturn in your fortune that such behavior brings.

In conclusion, the specific power call for communicating with Tyros is **SENTEN NAMU FURUHOBIRU**, while **UNTEN TOHBOH EHTAHTO** is the power call to use when asking the divine world of the North Star to keep you safe from harm or to bring you good luck.

HONBORA SOMOBIRU FURUFURUFURU, meanwhile, provides the enormous spiritual impetus which you will need if you are to keep the forces of evil at bay. So regardless of which power call you use for each specific circumstance, you can be sure that all three are certain to bring you significant advances in the quality of good fortune you enjoy.

THE FIFTH POWER CALL

Techniques to Maximize Your Capabilities

The fifth power call is an incantation designed to inspire your own spirit to achieve feats generally thought beyond you. It is

HARUCHI UMUCHI TSUZUCHI

HARUCHI UMUCHI TSUZUCHI ('haru-chi umu-chi tzuzu-chi') is the power call that Japanese gymnast Koji Gushiken used every time he entered a competition at the 1984 Los Angeles Olympics, where he went on to win a gold medal.

During a TV interview, Gushiken was asked about the incantation, and made the comment:

'If I use the incantation "Haruchi, Umuchi, Tsuzuchi", I feel that I can achieve whatever I set out to do. It gives me the faith to believe I can repeat the perfect work I do when I practice in the actual pressure of competition. And the fact is that happily things have turned out exactly as I believed they would.'

 I understand that Gushiken was taught this power call by his gymnastics coach — but this then poses the question, where did his teacher learn it? Actually, there are written records of the use of HARUCHI UMUCHI TSUZUCHI and its meaning found in a source well-known to all Japanese and those interested in the country's culture: none other than the *Kojiki (the Record of Ancient Matters)*.

The *Kojiki* is commonly accepted as the oldest historical book in Japan. It is a three-volume work written in *kambun* (Japanese written solely with Chinese characters), which is a mixture of myths, legends, and other ancient writings that form an initial reference point to many contemporary Japanese practices and beliefs. Historians suggest it was compiled around 1,400 years

ago, and the presence of this power call within the
scripts confirms that people of that time were familiar with its usage.

The 'Chi' in 'Haruchi' Means 'Blood'

Since ancient times, there has been a school of learning in
Japan known as *kotodamagaku* – which literally means the
'study of the spirit of words.' Broadly speaking, each and every
word we use is imbued with a divine presence, and each contains a profound meaning. Of course, the words of power calls
also reflect the will of the gods, which is why they manifest power
when you invoke them as an incantation.

This in turn raises the question: What is the will of the gods that
is secreted within the phrase HARUCHI UMUCHI TSUZUCHI? Let
us investigate that question from the standpoint of *kotodamagaku*.

When things are observed from the viewpoint of the divine and
spirit worlds, we can see that the blood that flows within the
bodies of human beings is, in fact, 'spirit' transformed into its
material form. Consequently, you might think of the situation in
terms of a person's entire spiritual essence being contained
within his blood. If a person's blood becomes polluted and he
becomes ill, then that will diminish the individual's spiritual power
and leave him vulnerable to possession by evil spirits. These

developments can be seen easily from the perspective of the spiritual realm, which also recognizes that the reverse can hold true: in many cases, after a person has undergone massive blood transfusions, his personality changes completely. This is an example of how the spiritual essences found in the blood of strangers can end up blending together and circulating through the body of an individual.

The word for blood in Japanese is *chi*. And the *chi* in the incantation HARUCHI UMUCHI TSUZUCHI refers to blood — where a person's blood amounts to his actual spirit. Having explained things so far, I think you can surmise that blood, as expressed in a component of this power call, is related to spiritual power.

If You Have Confidence, You Can Fulfill Your Latent Capabilities

Let me explain in a bit more detail the nature of this power call.

First, in looking at the construction of the word *'haruchi'*, the *'chi'* or 'blood' is seen to be *'haru'*. *'Haru'*, for its part, has the following connotations: 'development', 'expansion of power', the 'pushing out of one's chest', and the 'feeling of springtime'. In other words, it refers to the steady expansion outward, or blossoming, of power.

Next, let's turn to *'umuchi'*. This means that the blood is *'umu'*, which has the following connotations: 'give birth to children', 'become ripe', or 'produce things'. That is to say, it has as its meaning the act of production or creation.

Finally, we have *'tsuzuchi'*, which provides the meaning that blood is being *'tsuzumu'*. This verb has the following connotations: 'to stitch together', 'to be jammed together', 'to wrap up', 'to compress' or 'to collect' – as in 'collected water'. That is, it refers to something focused or concentrated, but with the potential for dispersal or fragmentation.

So what do we get when we put these three factors together? 'Developing' … 'giving birth to' … 'dispersal after solidification'. Through the study of the construction of these words it becomes apparent that the spirit and latent potential present in the blood flowing through our bodies possesses the meaning of 'development', 'birth', 'compression', and 'diffusion'.

If you use the power call HARUCHI UMUCHI TSUZUCHI, all the latent power that your spirit possesses has the potential to explode outward in one moment

---

If we consider these things from the standpoint of physiology, we know that if our blood is circulating well, then we feel healthy and strong, our thought processes seem finely attuned, and we adopt a positive attitude toward everything that we tackle. This is

Believe in These Words and Your Good Fortune Will Blossom

because both the body and spirit are operating at their full potential.

We can think of Gushiken's body before his performance in the Olympic stadium as being in a state of compressed potential. At the same time, he was saying to himself:

'I'm bound to succeed. I will achieve exactly what I set out to do in my performance.'

His faith in the outcome was profound, and he visualized his victory to such an extent that he became deeply convinced of the outcome.

Of course, it would be wrong to dismiss the huge contribution that his obsessive training and strength of character brought to Gushiken's victory, but by the same token it must also be recognized that without this spiritual facet to his preparation, his memorable victory would not have been possible.

I'm not very familiar with the sport of gymnastics, but I understand that competitors who reach world-class level are more or less equal in terms of sheer physical strength. The real deciding factors at this level are the competitors' physical and, more importantly, mental condition on the actual day of the competition – and whether or not they can bring out the full potential of their abilities under the pressure of a competition that represents the pinnacle of any gymnast's career.

Gushiken seems to have been well-aware of this situation. Therefore, he was particularly determined that in his hour of truth he would utter the power call with all the conviction he could muster.

Needless to say, this power call is not only for use by gymnasts: individuals in show business can use it before auditions, and, since this power call is a gift of the divine and spirit worlds of the moon, it also has a tremendous effect when it comes to dealing with friends or lovers. (The word for moon in Japanese is *tsuki*, which is close in sound to *tsukiai*, meaning 'to have human interaction'.)

For example, say that you are going on a date organized by a dating agency and you whisper HARUCHI UMUCHI TSUZUCHI prior to the meeting. If fortune has it that your future together would be a success, then the conversation will go very smoothly and you will enjoy each other's company. But if it would be an ill-fated match, then various obstacles will be thrown in your way, so that the date ends in failure and leaves you with no real desire to see that person again. We might say that here the power call represents a secret method for distinguishing which attachments are right for us.

The situation is similar in the world of commerce. When dealing with a new client, before getting down to business, it is best to turn to the power call for assistance. If the person you are tentatively dealing with would be a good long-term client, then your negotiations will proceed smoothly. If not, all kinds of problems will crop up and your prospective business arrangement will come to nothing.

This power call obviously has many very convenient applications, although it also has two important qualifications:

1 This approach will be worthless if the person using the power call is not sufficiently serious and humble when applying it.

2 You must support your use of the power call with your own common sense in appraising the situation.

The ideal approach to take in each situation lies in striking a suitable balance between reliance on common sense and the effectiveness of the power call.

Common Sense Techniques to Concentrate Willpower

Incidentally, while I was looking into Gushiken's case history, I discovered something quite interesting — it was that most sportsmen shared Gushiken's characteristic of using a method for concentrating their willpower. The method they employ is the height of simplicity and is immediately effective, and would seem to have a broad variety of applications beyond the world of sport. This is what they do.

First, they write down their specific goal on a piece of paper. For example, say a runner wants to run the 100 meters in 9.9 seconds. He writes that down, and then about two or three months before the actual race he writes 'I did it in 9.9 seconds,' and pins that up somewhere it will immediately catch his eye. If he does that, then inside his consciousness the

daily contact with the piece of paper creates a firm conviction that 'I did it in 9.9 seconds.' Of course, it goes without saying that during this build-up period he is also maintaining a very strict training regime aimed at bringing him to the peak of fitness at the right time.

Then, when it is a few days to the competition, he must visualize in his imagination a picture of himself actually running the 100 meters in 9.9 seconds.

'For the first 20 meters I will be in third place, with Maurice Green running just behind me. Since I know that he will make his move at around the 75-meter mark, I'm keeping something back in reserve. Well, now we're nearing that 75-meter mark. He's starting to pour it on, and so am I. But I'm inching ahead! Now we're giving it everything we've got as the tape rushes toward us. He's still a meter behind me. Finish line! I did it. I won. And my time was exactly as I predicted: 9.9 seconds ...'

The runner repeats this process many times over, setting the sequence of events firmly in his imagination. He never allows the intrusion of negative images or says to himself: 'I'll probably end up losing,' or 'I'll likely blow it at the start.' Instead, he always thinks positive, saying 'I can do it,' and 'I will do it.'

Finally, the day of the big race arrives. Since the runner has already done preparatory training countless times in his head, even as he takes his position at the starting line, he retains a firm inner conviction that 'I will run it in 9.9 seconds.' This helps him to remain relaxed as the tension mounts, and now all he has to do is run as he did in his visualizations.

Now if, just before the gun, our runner here did as Gushiken did before his big competition and turns to the power call for support, there is no question that he would put in a personal best performance.

So, if a competitor confidently says to himself: 'I will do it. It's as good as done,' he can feel confident that this unleashing of spiritual power, added to the hours of training and dietary discipline, will combine to produce a performance that demonstrates the full extent of his athletic potential.

完

Preventing Traffic Accidents

We never know when we might be unfortunate enough to be involved in an accident. Once it takes place, it is already too late to do anything about it. So although people who are familiar with the laws of the divine and spirit worlds should not be excessively cautious, it is also recommended that they use power calls before the fact to ensure they avoid the chance of becoming involved in any serious misfortune.

The thing to do is to choose the one that seems likely to be the most effective and appropriate in the given circumstances from among the five power calls I have already introduced, and then to place your utter faith in its abilities. To give an example: in order to guard yourself against traffic accidents (perhaps the most traumatic yet common of potential catastrophes we face), it is best to use the power call UNTEN TOHBOH EHTAHTO to help turn what could have been a disaster into eventual good fortune. If, at the same time, you employ the divine world logos to protect you, as explained in Chapter 5, then you should enjoy even more influence in this respect.

Even though I'm speaking of traffic accidents in general, the scope of resultant damage can differ considerably from accident to accident – everything from a minor shunt to horrific wrecks involving masses of twisted metal and multiple fatalities. Such painful and traumatic accidents are, sadly, a fact of our modern lives, and as such there are inevitably those unfortunate enough to fall into the categories of actually being responsible for those accidents and those who find themselves the innocent victims. It goes without saying that if possible, of course, all of us wish to find ourselves in neither category.

Happily, the power call UNTEN TOHBOH EHTAHTO is effective in ensuring this is the case, by reducing the seriousness of crashes that were originally destined to be major ones into only minor crashes, and even allows you to escape what were pre-destined to be minor crashes altogether.

That being so, when driving a motor vehicle, before putting on your seat-belt, take the time to perform a little safety procedure in your own heart by repeating to yourself the incantation UNTEN TOHBOH EHTAHTO.

Another power call that is potentially effective in these cases is the call SENTEN NAMU FURUHOBIRU, since it joins together the power of your guardian spirits to form a protective shield for you while on the road.

Occasionally you hear stories of how people manage incredible escapes from what appears to be certain death. But if such incidents are viewed from the perspective of the divine and spirit worlds, it becomes apparent that the people in question escaped harm principally because of the intervention of their guardian spirits. The problem then becomes not the actual circumstances of the near-death experience but, rather, how they deal with the aftermath.

Assume the person simply says to himself:

'Wow, that was really close. I think I'll go have a drink and calm myself down.'

Wouldn't that make the guardian spirits, who'd tried so hard to save his life, look rather pitifull and ignored? They might even feel insulted by his total ingratitude and promise to themselves,

'Well, that's the very last time we're going help him out of a tight spot.'

What the person who has been so remarkably lucky to be saved by his guardian spirits should, in fact, say is:

'Oh guardian spirits, thank you for pulling me out from danger. I promise to pay greater attention in the future, but, just in case, please keep looking out for me in the future as well.'

This is the very least he could do, and it probably also wouldn't hurt for him to clasp his hands together and give heartfelt thanks for his good fortune; for this is the proper way to give homage to your guardian spirits and the gods. If you follow this procedure, then your guardian spirits will be more than willing to protect you the next time you find yourself in difficulties. This is something definitely worth considering as, according to recent rumors I know to be rife among the guardian spirits, many of the guardian spirits and deities are regularly complaining that nowadays more and more people are increasingly loathe to give them their due respect in the proper form – and as a consequence they feel less and less inclined to lend their help.

Avoiding a Plane Destined to Crash

It is estimated that in 99 percent of airline crashes there are no survivors. Understandably, therefore, people want to avoid buying tickets for flights which are destined to end in a disaster of some kind, be it a crash, a hijacking or some other similarly heart-stopping incident. Such a natural desire consequently begs the question: How can we avoid such a fate?

The trick is to repeat the incantation HARUCHI UMUCHI TSUZUCHI when making your airline reservation. If you always remember to do this, then you will be blessed with the ability to avert a disaster before it happens. However, what should you do if you forgot to use the power call at the time you made your reservation, and then find yourself aboard a plane as it suddenly starts what appears to be a steep and irretrievable dive?

You might be unable to help yourself screaming,

'Save me. Save me. I don't care what happens to anyone else – just let ME live!'

But that would be a major mistake. This is making a transparently obvious statement that, in fact, you only care about your own personal welfare, with the result that the gods and spirits will probably end up making sure that you, and you alone, get it. They might, for example, cause luggage to fall from an overhead rack causing you a skull fracture, or allow you to be crushed in the rush to leave the plane after a safe emergency landing.

But you should handle things in the entirely opposite way, and pray to the gods and spirits in the following manner:

'UNTEN TOHBOH EHTAHTO. Please save us all. Please instruct me in the best way I can help the others and show me guidance to the very end on what is the best thing for me to do.'

In that case, you would be doing the right thing.

> The combination of the individual's strong will to survive and the desire to ensure others survive as well are both reflections of love

The divine and spirit worlds are likely to be deeply moved by these sentiments and will move to prevent the plane crashing.

If you should experience being on a plane in an emergency situation, the recommended course to take is to use the two power calls UNTEN TOHBOH EHTAHTO and HARUCHI UMUCHI TSUZUCHI in conjunction with each other. There are two reasons for this approach.

Firstly, in such a situation it is essential that you be able to focus all of the power within you right through to the very end — and not to adopt defeatist thinking in which you say to yourself, 'That's it, there's no way out of this, this is the end.' If you can continue to say to yourself, 'It's going to be okay, we're sure to be saved,' with all the willpower you can find in the very heart of

your soul, at that very instant you will be able to liberate the forces of 'saving good fortune', which will then be free to come to your aid.

Another reason is that, as you may recall, the power call HARUCHI UMUCHI TSUZUCHI is a gift from the moon world that promises to bring good luck to those who use it — so if you have already created a 'personal shield' of good fortune by using both these power calls, then there is further scope to use the force inherent in this power call to attract good fortune to the other passengers, and even to the fabric of the actual aircraft itself.

For example, what might happen is that a plane that is heading straight for a collision with a cliff will instead have its landing partially cushioned by trees growing on the mountain slope; or else it will have the unusual experience of floating on the surface of the sea for a considerable time after its crash landing; or perhaps the plane might even miraculously avoid crashing into a densely populated area and instead crash into an uninhabited rural area. Admittedly these examples are rather grim, but at least they demonstrate the relative benefits the power call brings to disasters that could have been much, much worse. In such cases, the plane would have been blessed with good luck that came as a direct result of your desire to do the right thing.

It is for these reasons that, if the plane you are on should suddenly go into a steep dive, it is strongly recommended that you use the two power calls UNTEN TOHBOH EHTAHTO and HARUCHI UMUCHI TSUZUCHI in tandem.

There have been cases in which 100 passengers were originally destined to die, but one of them invoked a power call, making it at least possible for five of them to survive certain death. Of course, the fortunes of the five individual survivors was no doubt quite strong to start with, but at the same time we can say that the power call used by one of those people was a very major contributory factor in saving their lives. These days, when it seems the papers are frequently filled with pictures of the latest air disaster, businessmen who frequently fly would be well-advised to memorize these two power calls to use as 'verbal amulets' while on their travels.

With Willpower You Can Pass that Exam

For young people an all too familiar, yet nevertheless important, aspect of their educational lives is the examination. As part of the education process we have to take all kinds of examinations: entrance exams, graduation exams, employment exams, mid-term tests, and term-end tests. The list just seems to go on and on. Just thinking about it makes my head throb!

School entrance exams and employment exams have great significance for an individual since they can determine the entire course of that person's life. Having studied for a number of years before the exam, those few hours of the actual examination are a time when it is essential that thorough preparation leads to a comprehensive and speedy outpouring of all the relevant information you have accumulated over the years of your education. And both your physical and mental condition on the day of the exam can be critical in shaping the quality of your performance – you should be in good physical shape, have a clear head, and have all the information carefully ordered within your memory.

In order to complete your preparation and leave you in a position where you are able to answer any question which may come up, you must make use of the 'secret willpower method',

as well as repeating the HARUCHI UMUCHI TSUZUCHI power call. I described in an earlier section the 'secret willpower method' (see page 140), but in this case you want to imagine that the score you're aiming for is pasted on the desk in front of you. Then you must say to yourself with genuine commitment, 'I have already achieved a pass score.'

Never allow yourself to think: 'Oh, I wonder if I really stand a chance,' for this does little more than promote negative thoughts and betray your resolve. Instead repeat to yourself: 'I'll take it, I'll take it, I'll take it. I can pass, I can pass, I can pass …' At the same time imagine yourself sailing through the questions, answering with ease one after the other. If at all possible, try to develop your level of conceptualization to the point that you can actually see the format of the questions as they appear on the test paper.

Even if your friends and acquaintances make fun of your attempts and reckon you'll never be able to pass the exam, don't give up. Just say, 'To hell with you' and redouble your efforts. Remember that, even though in daily life these people may be your friends, when you enter the examination room they often become your rivals. It's also important to remember not to let people know what you are up to by letting slip: 'I'm using the secret willpower method!' or 'I know a power call that is certain to make me pass!' Do so and you will foolishly sacrifice your self-confidence, and find yourself adversely influenced by the vengeful and evil spirits that have been attracted to the feelings of jealousy given off by your acquaintances – with the result that the methods you were depending on to help get you a pass score will end up doing you no good whatsoever.

Only after you get the pass grade you wanted will it be safe for you to tell your closest friends, and in the greatest of confidences, about the secrets of your success.

However, there are times when no matter how much you might have tried, you will still be unable to concentrate. At such times you may find yourself wanting to watch TV, read magazines, nibble on snacks, or just hang around with your friends – actions which represent evidence that evil spirits have come to visit you. In such a situation, repeat the power call SENTEN NAMU FURUHOBIRU and your guardian spirits will quickly protect you with their collective power. If at the same time you stare with conviction at the drawing of your band of guardian spirits, as detailed earlier, this will help to further increase the effectiveness of the power call.

How to Get Together
with Someone You Like

When a genuinely nice guy appeals to his guardian spirits with words like these: 'I really like that girl, but I'm so shy that I can't even talk to her,' I can guarantee that he will soon be provided with an opportunity to get to know her.

For example, they may see each other regularly at the bus stop and one day she might suddenly ask him the time; or as work colleagues she may even ask for his advice on some professional or personal problem; or they might both be ready to go home at the same time after work and she will unexpectedly say, 'How about catching a bite to eat?'

In order to be able to take advantage of such opportunities, and to maintain close contacts with one's guardian spirits, you need to make use of the power call SENTEN NAMU FURUHO-BIRU. After repeating this incantation, you should imagine your feelings being absorbed into the very lines, smudges and patches of whiteness that make up the sketch of your band of guardian spirits, and then make your appeal. Although you might be unable to confess your feelings in front of the girl in question, you can feel free to say anything in front of your own band of guardian spirits. You might say:

'I really like Julia, but I have no idea whether she likes me or

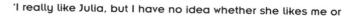

not. If she thinks I'm at least okay, then please guide me in such a way that we can become closer. I promise to do my best to make sure that it will be for the welfare of, not just myself, but Julia too. So please help me out. If at all possible, please provide me with a chance to talk to her later this week.'

It is best to set a clear time limit for your request, as usually you will have the benefit of seeing your request satisfied within that limit. But should the period expire without you getting what you asked for, just make the request again but this time without a time limit – it is important that you keep on trying indefinitely until you get the results you're after.

You should repeat this power call a total of 36 times before, and with the smiling face of Julia still pictured clearly in your mind, you address her guardian spirits in the following way:

'Guardian spirits and guardian deities of Julia, please look kindly upon me.'

Say this 10 times. Since the use of this power call will cause the guardian spirits to work in unison, it is possible to influence, not just your own guardian spirits, but also the guardian spirits of the object of your affection.

However, there is one important point that I should draw your attention to: do not use this power call if your motives are not genuine. In saying that, let me qualify it by giving you some specific examples. Do not use it if all you're thinking is, 'I'm going to make Julia my own little plaything,' or 'I'm going to look really cool walking down the street with Julia by my side,' since the divine and spirit worlds detest nothing more than a power call used to further such rampant egotism.

If your request is fuelled by selfish intentions, it will be denied

---

To make matters worse, the power call may even attract the wrath of Heaven into the bargain.

On the other hand, if you choose to use the power call properly, you stand a more than 90 percent chance of having your request to get to know the person you like better granted. And if that person is fairly ambivalent toward you, then the chances rise to a 100-percent certainty that your guardian spirits will arrange a meeting – although after that, of course, it comes down to your own abilities to see if you can persuade that person to continue to spend time with you!

As I said, whether everything goes smoothly after that initial meeting depends largely on your own powers. However in order to ensure you don't find yourself in a situation where you are simply too tense to even speak, you can turn to the power call

HARUCHI UMUCHI TSUZUCHI, or the 'secret willpower method', to provide help in making sure the meeting goes according to plan.

In any event, the most important factor in this whole process is whether your own motives are both genuine and honestly expressed. So in order to make sure that you don't become all flustered and make a mess of things when the moment of truth arrives, make a few notes of what you want to say, so that when nerves do begin to get the better of you, you will still have an instant point of reference that clearly lists what you want to say.

This method is appropriate for making friends of all kinds and not just for meeting prospective love partners, so I would strongly encourage those of you who wish to widen your circle of friends to feel happy using this power call on a regular basis.

How to Heal a Broken Heart

What can you do if you encounter deep unhappiness, where the person that you love rejects you?

All kinds of thoughts begin racing through our minds, everything from morbid self-pity, to twisted thoughts of anguished revenge:

'Oh, I feel so utterly miserable. Why did she have to go and dump me? Oh, guardian spirits I truly wish you could cause her the same kind of pain I'm going through.'

However these kind of sentiments are the worst kind you can allow yourself to foster. It is not that I don't understand that people, in their despair, sometimes feel the need to say things like this, but if you wish bad things on other people, that 'intention' will then be transformed into an *ikiryo*, or 'living wraith', which is destined to cause unhappiness either for the other person or for yourself.

These *ikiryo* are malevolent spirits, forged from the corrupted emotions of living human beings, and who within the powers of their existence possess an extremely potent spiritual force capable of sometimes inflicting even death on their intended victims. I still often remember how a college friend of mine split up with the girl he was due to marry in a painful and ill-tempered argument. Her desire for revenge then became so obsessive that it ended up fostering a female *ikiryo* that was ultimately responsible for taking away his young, and what we all saw as a hugely promising, life.

Furthermore, the person responsible for creating an *ikiryo* actually loses part of his own spirit in the process, and in the most extreme of cases can actually die himself as a result of his negative desires. Therefore, be careful to neither create 'living wraiths' nor allow yourself to become possessed by them. There are notable exceptions however – there are certain cases in which good intentions, which are not merely the product of a stubborn or inflexible love, can also become *ikiryo*. They are created by pure feelings, which desire only good and selfless benefits for the object of their devotion. It may be that they wish the person long-lasting happiness, or want to make sure they are protected from harm, or that they may find true love even if it is not with the person involved in making the appeal. These particular *ikiryo* will then actually protect and bring happiness to the person toward whom such tender sentiments are directed.

Well then, what is the best strategy to adopt when you have been rejected by the one you love? To be quite frank, it is best that you just accept the situation for what it is – although of course that is something easier said than done. But in order to make that task a little easier, let me offer some practical methods for dealing with such a situation.

❶ Begin to recognize the reality that your two personalities are fundamentally ill-matched and that if you continue to interact with each other as you are doing now, you will both end up unhappy. End the affair with a clear finality, and do not read any love letters or reply to any communication that you may receive from her.

② Assure yourself that you have acted in complete good faith throughout the course of the relationship – something which your guardian spirits will readily recognize – and pray for the happiness of your former partner. If you do that then your guardian spirits will be more inclined to help you find a more suitable partner, while you can also find comfort in the knowledge that your truly genuine sentiments will be converted into a wealth of good virtue that will be waiting for you when your time comes to join the spirit worlds.

③ Spend time recalling the days of your youth, forming within your mind a picture of the vast wealth of happy and varied events your life has contained so far. This will enable you to position the trauma of your broken relationship within the greater perspective of your past life, helping it to look less significant. This will allow you to think more positively about how you are going to begin creating a new life for yourself in the immediate future.

Use these three methods and I guarantee you will soon be well on your way to healing the pain caused by your lost love.

Of course it is easy to write about such things

from an objective position, but a person who finds himself in such a situation suffers in a way that others can only partially understand. So if a person looks at these techniques but still convinces himself

'With the desolation I feel right now, there's just no way this is going to make me feel any better,'

there is little more to be done with him. At this point it is probably best to let the person help relieve their grief in a long flood of tears. In fact, it is amazing how a good cry for a couple of hours can leave a person unexpectedly refreshed and better prepared to face the situation. If you doubt the truth of this, then on the sad occasion when you do find your own heart has been broken, simply give this method a try and discover the truth of it for yourself. The point here is not to just sit there and sob quietly, but to really purge your sadness in a long, hard cry. Directing your tears toward Tsukiteruhiko no Okami – the ruling God of the Moon – will also help, as within his range of powers he has the ability to bring a sense of calm and peace to broken hearts.

Using Failure in Love as the Launch Pad for Garnering Good Luck

When someone you like features heavily in your dreams, and as long as that person is not tainted with ill fortune, then you can look forward in the knowledge that opportunities to work positively to improve your destiny and your situation in general will soon present themselves. These improvements will apply not only to your love-life, but to whatever aspect of your life you're currently heavily involved with — and will bring with them corresponding improvements in your own happiness.

But what happens when you encounter problems? After all, none of us is free from the occasional unfortunate setback.

How we react to disappointments has a tremendous influence upon how our luck develops in the future

---

In the case of lost love, the three techniques I described above are the most appropriate way to react to the situation and to begin healing the pain. We should never bear ill-feelings against our former partners or lose faith in the positive nature of our own destiny, since, if we can do this, our guardian spirits are certain to bring us an alternative form of good luck that will lead us in new and equally challenging directions.

More specifically, you may discover significant improvements in your academic grades, or you may even meet someone who quickly reveals themselves to be a more compatible and desirable partner than the one you just broke up with. Out of the blue, someone you had hardly even noticed before will suddenly confess, 'I really like you!' and when something like that happens, even a heart that before seemed terribly hurt will quickly feel lightened and ready to face a bright and promising future. We can call this the 'Method for Recovering 10-fold from the Pain of Lost Love.'

The same principle applies to all kinds of other situations. Say you fail an important exam, or you have a quarrel with your friend, and you generally feel that things are not working out as you had originally planned. If you then refuse to allow yourself to wallow in your own self-pity, but instead maintain the strength to forge ahead, your guardian spirits will respect your efforts and bring the Goddess of Good Fortune to your side to help you in your endeavors.

For that reason, especially when you find yourself on the painful end of a failed relationship, you should regard it as a crossroads in your life that needs to be successfully negotiated. If you continue in a forward-oriented direction, the Goddess of Good Fortune will be waiting for you along the way with a banquet of good fortune and happiness — but if you make a turn that takes you along a path characterized by thoughts of regret and revenge, evil spirits will be lying in wait to hijack what remains of your good fortune. Your guardian spirits and the evil spirits will both be doing their very best to entice you along their respective routes, but it remains up to the individual to make that ultimate decision as to which path to take.

Seek Revenge and Say Good-bye to Luck

Earlier I discussed the problem of *ikiryo* or 'living wraiths'. But here let me explain exactly how your good fortune can be gradually sapped if, by choosing the path of regret and retribution, you thereby encourage the creation of such demons.

If you bear resentment and ill feelings toward another person, you badly disrupt the spiritual vibrations that emanate constantly from your own person.

Mental disruption and unease will result in your character becoming more irrational and prone to anger, with a resultant decrease in your powers of concentration

---

When you exist in a situation where your emotions are in this kind of unstable flux, the resultant behavior patterns also display a tendency toward manic depression: radical mood-swings which fluctuate between the extremes of deep depression and irrational cheerfulness.

These behavior patterns can be explained by the idea that thoughts of revenge serve to attract evil spirits in a similar way to the way a magnet attracts metal. Moreover, this initial creation of *ikiryo* spirits often results in a longer-lasting legacy, where their presence can lead to a malignant corruption of part or parts of your own inner spiritual self.

The situation is analogous to a fly burying itself in a bowl of freshly cooked rice. No one would want to touch such tainted food, and similarly both guardian spirits and the gods themselves avoid people who are recognized as being touched by evil. So once they choose to abandon someone, then it logically follows that his luck is certain to take a radical downturn.

However, if a person reflects conscientiously upon the state of his emotions, and then resolves to modify the inappropriate ones, then at that very moment of decision the evil spiritual presences will vacate their host and disappear in search of a more appropriate target.

The stronger a grudge you bear against someone, the more inclined evil spirits will be to gather around your person, slyly

 evaluating your potential as a worthy host. In extreme cases, they might even combine their separate entities to form a giant *ikiryo* with an independent existence of its own.

> The scale of resentment and the degree of positive destiny are in direct inverse proportion. This is an iron rule of the divine and spirit worlds – the stronger the grudge, the poorer the luck

If You Pray Half-heartedly, You Will Not Enjoy Success

It is perfectly understandable that someone who has actually seen their fortune improve through the use of the power calls would also like to see other people take advantage of their miraculous power. But there is a danger inherent in this attitude, because unless the person who has benefited from use of the power calls completely believes that the power manifested in them derives from the spiritual world, then it becomes totally inappropriate for them to employ the calls or to teach them to others. If a person was to do so without communicating the entire spirit behind the power calls, it would lead to catastrophic results.

For example, if in a case where the person uses the unifying power call SENTEN NAMU FURUHOBIRU or, in order to nullify a curse, the call HONBORA SOMOBIRU FURUFURUFURU, he may well be able to drive away the evil spirits afflicting him and see a radical improvement in his luck. But if he was then to invite his friends to his home and try to improve their fortune in the same way, it would be completely unacceptable.

It is perfectly fine for an individual to memorize and use the power calls for his own needs, but if he is willing to allow another person to attempt to improve his luck for him, then he is liable to end up under the control of that other person's evil spirits. The reason for this is that the strength of the person's will is insufficient to repel the influence of external evil spirits that have been indirectly invited to approach you by your friend's ill-advised actions.

Good fortune is a treasured gift from the divine and spirit worlds; treat it neither lightly nor with a lack of suitable respect

---

If good fortune is not properly respected, it just invites suffering, and not just now but beyond the boundaries of life. After all, the powers inherent in the spiritual world are the forces which bind

our physical bodies to our eternal souls, and as such should never be treated as a plaything. They should instead only be used with a pure heart, and without ever losing sight of the fundamental principles of honor and gratitude.

THE CORRECT WAY TO USE THE POWER CALLS

Frame of Mind

1. Rid your mind of any doubts, and firmly believe that the power call you are using is completely effective.
2. Never use a power call to do wrong. Do so and the gods are certain to exact severe punishment.
3. Do not avoid the hard work that forms an essential component of your desired goals.
4. Maintain a spirit of dogged perseverance until your desire is finally satisfied.

Environment

1. Avoid noisy places where you are unable to focus your spiritual self.
2. Turn off the TV, radio or any similar distractions in the room.
3. Do not perform the power call in total darkness – such circumstances tend to attract evil spirits.

4 Never invoke a power call at around 3.00 a.m. as evil spirits are often most active around this time.

5 Maintain a clean environment, enabling you to function in a fresh and invigorating atmosphere.

Attitude

1 It does not matter whether your eyes are open or closed.

2 It is best to have your hands clasped in prayer in front of your face when employing a power call, although not absolutely necessary. The primary concern is comfort when invoking the power calls.

3 Say out loud exactly what you want, and if your wishes do come true then do not forget to express your gratitude in an appropriate manner.

Power Calls Results

Power Calls	Results
Senten Namu Furuhobiru	All kinds of good spirits will gather in a collective band, with your guardian spirits as the nucleus, to back you up. At the same time, you will also be able to unite with your guardian spirits. As a result, you will be able to tap into and be influenced by the natural spiritual essence from Heaven and Earth
Nohmakusahmanda Bahzaradansenda Bahzaradansenda Makaroshada Sowataya Untara Takanman (*shorter version: Nohmakusahmanda Bazaradankan*)	Fudo Myoo, who possesses enormous willpower and strength, will become the core of your band of guardian spirits. As a result, the power of the spirit band, including your guardian spirits, will grow three-fold

Believe in These Words and Your Good Fortune Will Blossom

Unten Tohboh Ehtahto

Say this power call while looking at a divine world good fortune logo mark and disaster will be transformed into happiness

Haruchi Umuchi Tsuzuchi

Your latent powers will well up in an astonishing fashion

Honbora Somobiru Furufurufuru

This is a simple form of exorcism. It is guaranteed to be effective when it comes to removing invisible spiritual chains

Amaterasu Ohmikami *(also known as the* 'tokoto no kajiri')

Repeat this power call 11 times and the power of the sun will bathe your path of progress

THE TRUE
MEANING OF
'PRAYING TO
THE STARS'

STARS – SYMBOLS OF DESTINY AND FORTUNE

Since ancient times, mankind has placed great faith in the practice of 'astrology'. At night people would turn their eyes to the heavens and seek within the patterns that the stars wove across the darkness some sign of what the future held for them.

Nowadays, we have tended to relegate the predictive powers of the stars more to the realms of whimsy, and instead place greater faith in the sciences to explain our existence and to chart our destinies. But in ancient times, when scientific civilization had not reached the level that it has today, people looked upon the sun, moon, and North Star with a deep reverence, and were ultra-sensitive to messages carried by the breath of nature about their fates and fortunes. Their communion with the stars formed a hugely important and integral part of their lifestyles. However, as the millennia progressed and civilization flourished, astrology came to be considered unscientific, and was relegated to little more than an amusing pastime.

For people who will only believe what they can see with their own eyes, the idea that spiritual emanations from the sun, moon, and North Star reach us here on Earth, or that there are deities and spirits living on those celestial bodies, would seem simply unbelievable.

Of course, there is no denying that the stars do not have a harmonious balance of air and water (such as we have here on

Earth), that would make life possible. The sun, for example, is a super-hot world with temperatures of tens of thousands of degrees centigrade. It has neither an atmosphere nor water, nor does it know the difference between day and night. Or take the moon, the closest heavenly body to Earth. It exists in an almost perfect vacuum, while the other heavenly bodies that surround us are

no doubt the same – worlds with bleak, harsh, and forbidding environments. So, it might seem reasonable to ask why the gods and spirits would purposely choose such uninviting locations as their dwelling places. But a more-than superficial study of the issue would reveal how wrong it is to assume that such worlds are barren places, merely because they do not conform to what we recognize on Earth as a hospitable environment.

The people of ancient times were able to hear messages from the stars by baring their souls to the heavens and dedicating all their powers of concentration to receiving and then interpreting these emanations. And these abilities are not something which were exclusive to people from ancient times – although largely unpracticed, the same skills still exist today if we choose to revive and hone them. It is worth noting here that almost all the people who have accompanied me on my regular 'star tours' have been able to witness such extra-terrestrial communication through the 'eyes of their spirit' – what I refer to as their *kushimi-tama* soul.

The Triple Structure of Heavenly Bodies

Careful research conducted over many years has revealed to me that the structure of the star worlds strongly resembles the structure of the human body, once it is analyzed within the concept of a 'three-tier structure'.

An analysis of the body based on the principle of a three-tier structure will be a novel idea to most of you, but is based upon a thorough knowledge of the relationship between the physical and the spiritual. The 'exterior' of the human body is represented by our flesh; inside that outer casing, within the 'interior', resides our spirit; while at the very 'core' of our being is our *kushimitama* soul. In this case, the 'exterior' and 'interior' of the body are not in a simple three-dimensional relationship — it is rather a case of the body or 'flesh' existing within a three-dimensional state, while the spirit actually has a fourth-dimensional existence, and the *kushimitama* extends to an even higher-dimensional plane.

A comfortable understanding of this idea enables you to draw direct parallels with the structure of the star worlds, which follow essentially the same system: the celestial bodies that we can see through a telescope correspond to the physical part of human beings, but the inner parts corresponding to the spirit and the *kushimitama* remain invisible.

> What human beings cannot see with their eyes, they must
> see with their spirits or their *kushimitama* souls

A detailed discussion of the stars follows in the next section, but here let me just note that human beings without physical bodies – in other words the form we take prior to rebirth – dwell on the celestial bodies most appropriate to their spiritual state at that time. They spend hundreds of years in these places undergoing spiritual training, before they are either reborn as human beings or move up to take residence in the next level of the star world.

Experiencing the Star Worlds through 'Star Tours'

As mentioned earlier, when the spiritual component of people and the celestial power of the stars react well together, the product is an exceptionally rich reward of good fortune. I also explained how there are various methods for achieving such a positive interaction, including using power calls, increasing willpower, and inviting the assistance of your guardian spirits. However, even when employing these techniques, the results will still vary depending upon the extent of the individual's knowledge of what is actually going on in the spiritual dimension of the star worlds, and how he is to receive in the most appropriate manner the spiritual power given off by these star worlds.

The quickest way to truly appreciate what is happening in those worlds is to employ a technique that enables you to leave our living world in a temporary, deathlike state, and to actually go and see what is happening there. But this approach is not possible for everyone; in fact it is only in rare cases that special permission is granted by the divine and spirit worlds to make such a journey.

In earlier times, people who could freely make trips to the star worlds were referred to as 'prophets' or 'servants of the gods'

These travelers included such world-renowned illuminati as Nostradamus, Emanuel Swedenborg, and Onisaburo Deguchi. Yet all that these 'prophets' really did was to freely travel to and from the star worlds, from the perspective of which they were able to view the past and future of mankind. When they came back to tell their fellow human beings what they had seen, to the average person their words seemed to take on the same prophetic qualities as if they were the words of the gods themselves.

It can therefore be confirmed that journeys to the star worlds bring both tremendous improvements in your fortunes and the ability to know about the past and the future – but regardless of how much a person may want to make such a journey, the ability to do so depends upon permission being granted by the spiritual world of the stars.

It certainly seems unfair that only a handful of people are blessed with this permission, and I consider myself very fortunate to be included in such an auspicious group. In an attempt to share my good luck with others, I regularly conduct 'star tours' with a strictly controlled number of participants, who are all guaranteed to come back from

a journey that examines the past, the future, and the happenings of the spirit worlds, completely unharmed.

Although my having to directly lead any group on a 'star tour' necessitates imposing a limit on its numbers, there is no need to become depressed at the thought that you will be unable to directly experience the star worlds. It is fundamental to remember that the stars give off tremendous spiritual power, which in turn directly influences our spiritual selves and the direction our destinies take, and so all we have to do is achieve a spiritual awakening *(satori)* to this fact in order to achieve greater control over the direction our lives take.

In the next section I will introduce you to a number of special images which help portray the relevant properties of the stars, and explain how you can use these to recreate the images of the star worlds within your inner being. However, first I would like to describe a little of what a 'star tour' actually entails.

The key component of a person that goes on the star tour is the one of the four 'souls' that every human being has with the most central, fundamental existence – namely the *kushimitama* that I discussed earlier. This 'soul' enters the body and exists in the spot commonly referred to as the 'third eye'. In the language of yoga, this spot is referred to as the *ajani*, or 'chakra': it is the point that holds the flesh and spirit together. (I introduce the nature of the *kushimitama* on page 215)

We usually have about ten participants when we depart on a star tour, although when I say 'depart', all that this actually demands is for the participants to sit and relax in chairs and gently close their eyes. They then fold their hands in front of their chests, in a room which should be kept quiet and dimly lit so as not to disturb concentration.

Next, I concentrate all of my willpower and attempt to draw out the *kushimitama* from the head of each one of my fellow travelers. Here, sorry to say, if a person's thoughts are not entirely focused, it will create a hardened 'shell' around the head that makes it impossible for the person's *kushimitama* to exit. In such cases, I sometimes resort to using the spiritual equivalent of a chisel or plane, and on occasions even a large hammer to crack open this hard shell!

During this process many of the participants mention a sensation of deep heat centered around the forehead – a phenomenon caused by the flow of the spiritual power which exerts a subtle influence upon their physical bodies.

A star tour lasts about 20 minutes at the longest, and during this time the participants do not have any thoughts of their own, but rather witness images floating through their minds which appear to be the products of a separate 'consciousness'. These images are actually the scenes of the star worlds, as experienced by the *kushimitama*.

After becoming accustomed to such experiences, it is possible to repeat trips to the star worlds through impromptu moments of concentration and without need for a dedicated room or the comfort of silence. There are even some people who enjoy a mastery of this technique to such an extent that they are able to freely discuss the future and the past with the supreme god of any given star – in much the same way as Nostradamus and Onisaburo Deguchi did in their time.

Several hundred people have already experienced my star tours. In many cases, although a person may not experience any significant images on his first 'flight', after one or two more attempts vivid images begin to slowly filter into the person's consciousness. A typical star tour involves visits to three or four planetary bodies; usually starting with the moon, we progress to

Mercury and then Jupiter – although most visions usually come as we reach the last of our destinations. I have not kept any detailed statistics in this regard, but I would estimate that in more than 95 percent of cases, participants share some kind of common images of the star worlds that we visit. And in many cases, closely following their involvement in the star tour, these people will unexpectedly experience an improvement in the quality of their luck, a fresh burst of artistic inspiration, or some other development which brings direct benefit to their lives. It is for this reason that many musicians, writers, and similarly artistic individuals tend to be especially keen to participate in these star tours.

VIBRATIONS FROM THE STARS THAT INVITE GOOD LUCK

Good Fortune from the Stars is Available to Anyone

At this point I would like to explain certain aspects of the star worlds for those of my readers who will never have the chance to participate in one of the star tours, and to describe the proper frame of mind you should adopt if you wish to attract the powers of positive destiny by praying to the stars. It is essential that you understand the correct procedure involved, because if you approach it with the wrong attitude you will be unable to take fullest advantage of the good-fortune powers that reach down from the stars.

For example, let us take the case of the sun. It shines with a piercing brightness that damages the eyes if looked at directly, and with a vibrant radiation that bathes the ground in warmth. And when we feel the delicious sensation of the sun warming our skin as we look up to the sky with closed eyelids, few of us can fail to appreciate the power the sun has to both provide us with life and to influence the way we feel.

People who always seem to have good fortune within their grasp before eventually seeing it disappear tend to be people who only consider the material side of the sun. On the other hand, individuals who consistently enjoy good luck are fundamentally different: in most cases, they are able to appreciate both the sun's material and spiritual aspects. The spiritual aspects I am speaking of here are those aspects of the sun that transcend mere considerations of its physical presence – the burning gases, the massive gravitational forces – but recognize the non-physical factors which exist beyond these mere superficial ones.

Let me offer a simple explanation of this point.

For example, if you find yourself bathed in the sun's warmth and light, you are far more likely to adopt the go-ahead attitude which says, 'Okay then. No messing around now – let's do this thing!' which shows that you are allowing yourself to be strongly influenced by the good-fortune power of the sun. Such influences go far beyond the physical concerns of heat and light, and point instead to the existence of fourth and fifth-dimension spirit worlds of the sun, which also (in another separate but related function), act as the controlling 'central government' for the spirit and divine worlds of the other bodies which make up our Solar System.

When we see the glory of the rising sun, we are often likely to feel our hearts begin to beat that fraction faster. This reaction, and ones like it, are direct results of the good-fortune power of the sun, which is absorbed into our bodies through various channels such as the eyes, mouth, nose, ears, and even the very pores of our skins. And as a result of this absorption, we enjoy a feeling of refreshment and renewed vitality owed to powers from the sun far greater than its mere light and heat.

During the day this power is also slowly absorbed into the earth beneath us, while during the night this power, contained within an earth that acts as some huge kind of global solar-power reservoir, still remains available to be drawn into our bodies.

> What we define as a 'lucky person' is someone who is unconsciously aware of the constant availability of this good-fortune power from the sun, and who readily taps into it during the course of his life

It should be borne in mind that the sun is not exclusively capable of projecting power toward the Earth – similar forms of power are also radiated from the moon, the other neighboring planets, and the vast myriad of stars which stretch far beyond our Solar System.

People with 'naturally endowed' talents are those who can perceive this benevolent power being radiated from the stars and take advantage of it whenever they can. Conversely, people who are unable to recognize this incredible power and allow it to just pass them by, fall into a trap whereby they find themselves unable to succeed no matter what they attempt to do. The kind of attitude required to take advantage of the good fortune inherent in the stars demands that there is no absent-minded gazing at the sun, moon or stars, but rather a look of focused faith which clearly says:

'There is indeed something there which stretches beyond the mere physical – I can feel the positive power and waves of their good fortune gently washing over me.'

If you can do this, the spirit worlds that have recognized and absorbed your thoughts will develop the kind of internal personal consciousness that will be translated into overt displays of their spiritual power, and which are in turn available for you to harness in order to shape the course of your own destiny.

Advantages in Certain Stars

First of all, let me introduce the types of good-fortune power given off by the various stars. I have been authorized to do so by the divine and spirit worlds, but would stress that this is not a comprehensive list – they are, however, the most important in ranking, and are quite sufficient in number for you to take advantage of in the course of your everyday life.

THE SUN

The sun is an extremely bright, highly active celestial body, without which most of the plant and animal life on Earth simply could not exist. In fact, the sun is recognized as the ultimate source of all life, and in the spiritual sense too, it occupies the role of an unrivaled source of energy and influence.

Bearing this in mind, you will find that if you can form a positive attitude to life that encourages you to always strive to be the best person you possibly can be, a deep instinct will develop within you which recognizes the primal significance of the sun and the nature of its relationship with you as a human being. Since the sun stands at the center of the Solar System, playing the role of 'central government', it also exerts a very real influence upon our relationship with the other planets and celestial bodies which revolve around it.

The sun is also home to 64 separate communities, which directly mirror, or correspond to the sacred places of various ethnic groups and nation states that we have here on Earth. You can think of the sun as having a direct impact on what happens here on Earth via the decisions that are made by each of these separate communities.

The deity said to be responsible for general supervision of the activities of these communities is Amaterasu Ohmikami, the Goddess of the Sun – while the official Supreme Deity of the sun is Amaterasu Ohirumemuchi, who exercises the actual hands-on control of these 64 communities.

The official name for Amaterasu Ohmikami, when written using Chinese characters, makes it clear that she is a female deity: one who is normally depicted in pictures wearing elegant clothes of deep crimson. She is worshipped at the Hinomisaki Shrine in the ancient area of Izumo, located on the coast of Japan's main island of Honshu, where her accepted image has been passed down from generation to generation, dating back to her appearance before the inhabitants of the 'Kingdom of

Yamato' of ancient Japan. However, if you go to the Parthenon in Athens, a shrine dedicated to the goddess Athena, you will see that Athena, who is actually an alternative representation of the same goddess, is dressed in an elegant pure white dress. In her respective forms, both in Greece and Japan, she embodies all the sophistication, elegance, and refinement of the most beautiful woman on Earth. Whenever I go to the divine world of the sun, I make a point of visiting her temple to offer worship to her.

It is not strictly true to say that Amaterasu Ohmikami rules the sun spirit world alone, as she is helped in her task by two other deities: Amenotokotachi no kami and Kuniharutachi no kami. Although the name of the former is found in numerous sacred Shinto scriptures, it is not clear to me where he lived on Earth – although I do know that he was an impressive white-bearded figure, whose alternative representation in the Greek pantheon would be the god Apollo. The latter, Kuniharutachi no kami, is the 'God of Life', whom I have witnessed on many occasions casting 'seeds of life' (which resemble small sapphires), down to Earth from his home in the sun spiritual world.

In our three-dimensional world the sun appears as a fiery globe, burning at unimaginable temperatures, and upon which no life as we recognize it could possibly exist. But as I have already explained, stars such as the sun actually exist on three different planes, and the fiercely burning sphere that lights up

our world represents only one of those planes.
Besides this existence that is clearly visible to the
human eye, there are others which exist beyond
mere material considerations – and it is these
ultra-dimensional existences of the sun that correspond directly to the dimensions of the heart
and the *kushimitama* soul of human beings.

An important point to remember here is to use
the full and correct names of the three central
deities when praying to the sun divine world. If
you can pronounce the names of these deities
correctly and with genuine sincerity, the vocal
sounds you produce will resonate more truly with the depth of
your feelings; with the result that you will be better able to
encourage the gods to work on your behalf.

If I were to try to give very detailed descriptions of the sun
divine and spirit worlds it would, without doubt, have a greater
impact on my readers. But, unfortunately, their scale is such that
a detailed description alone, without even examining the varied
other aspects and associated issues intrinsically involved in
these worlds, would easily fill an entire book.

As I noted earlier, the goddess Amaterasu Ohmikami exercises
overall control over all developments in the sun divine world –
and to her you should, in a very careful and clearly enunciated
style, direct the power call known as TOKOTO NO KAJIRI (a repe-
tition of the name 'AMATERASU OHMIKAMI' and pronounced

'tock-oto no kadg-iri'), and repeat it 11 times. You might also try recounting the following powerful religious song.

Oh, ye three rulers of the Sun,
Shower down the light of your beings to show us the path of
*   happiness and good fortune.*
Oh, ye three rulers of the Sun,
Who govern over the actions of the myriad celestial gods,
We are confident that if we most humbly and diligently pray,
Ye gods on high will shed your beneficent light on us.

(Toshu Fukami)

MERCURY

Because Mercury is relatively close to the sun when compared to the Earth, the sun's rays are particularly strong as they enter its atmosphere, and its spiritual inhabitants therefore have to wear large hats to protect themselves from their severity. I was fortunate enough to be told by its ruling god that there are about one billion people there, and that in terms of its spiritual level, it occupies a position a little higher than the average within the mid-level spirit-world range. I was informed that this is the world where people who have lived good, common sense lives while on Earth are transported to after death.

If the planets in the Solar System were to be compared to the various stages in a human being's life, then Mercury would corre-spond to the early childhood years between the ages of about three and five. It evokes very clear and simple feelings that correspond well to those of a child at that age, when their desire for knowledge is developing quickly and they are forever asking, 'Why? Why?'. Thus, Mercury can be seen to send waves of cosmic energy toward the Earth's surface which, once absorbed by our bodies, then stimulates us in what forms one of the primary driving forces of our consciousness: to seek the numerous, elusive, and sometimes multi-faceted forms of 'truth' which litter our complex lives, and the societies in which we function.

That being the nature of this planet's divine and spirit worlds, it is advisable for those with special interest in a subject, or those with great ambitions who wish to pursue them further, to turn toward Mercury in order to make use of the valuable spiritual energy that constantly emanates from it. Mercury is also home to Daikoku (Mahakala), the 'God of Wealth', who is one of the seven ancient deities of good fortune.

If you want to acquire wisdom on economic matters and to apply that wisdom in commercial ventures, it is best to direct your prayers to Mercury

Having been the first person to clarify the role of Toyotamahime no kami, wife of the planet's ruling god, I can assure you that she is in fact the best deity to pray to when seeking help in matters of self-esteem or luck in economics. If you are subsequently successful in business you should attribute it to the intervention of this goddess who, although her name appears on ancient scriptures, had until my recent insight occupied a unknown role within the functions of this planet.

VENUS

The image of Venus appears from time to time in numerous religious works, crossing many boundaries of thought and doctrine. And in a similar way to the explanation given of Mercury, the period of human life to which it corresponds is that time of young adulthood which extends from the age of 18 to the age of 25: a critical period in a person's development usually characterized by expectant potential accompanied by a surfeit of raw energy. If you find yourself troubled by problems related to your financial situation, your artistic aspirations, or even issues of a religious nature, then it is toward the spiritual world of Venus that I recommended your prayers be primarily directed.

Since the spirit of this planet corresponds to the period of a person's young adulthood, it also follows that the spiritual character of the planet is generally distinguished by a passionate willingness to challenge and overcome anything that stands in its way.

During these years – what we might call the springtime of thought – human beings are greatly influenced by both Mercury and Venus, whose influences play a very significant role in the development of the psychological and spiritual sides of our personalities. In fact, the course our lives are destined to take is usually decided by the actions of Venus during this period; a time when we are also most likely to undergo a change of guardian spirits (something which in its own respect, of course, contributes greatly to determining the direction our lives are to take).

Because of their tendency to mature a year or two earlier than men, it's also worth noting that young women begin to experience the increasing influence of Venus not from the age of 18, but a year, or sometimes even two, earlier.

When viewed from the perspective of the divine worlds, Venus is considered one of the high-level spirit worlds, where it occupies a place just below the sun divine world. People who have been successful in the world of religion come here after their deaths – although when I say 'people who have been successful,' I refer not to the number of their followers or their degree of fame, but to their ability to remain free of any preoccupation with dogma, their ability to love their neighbors in a broadly religious sense, and their consistent preaching of the proper road to take to those who wished to listen.

The universally religious significance of this planet, and its function as a conduit for religious doctrines and rules sent from the divine and spirit worlds, can be further illustrated by its relevance to a number of religious incidents which shaped respective religious movements.

The 'shining star' that Buddha was looking at when he achieved the 'enlightenment' that said we are one with heaven and earth, and it is only our egos that cause us to isolate ourselves, was the planet Venus

---

When Moses led the children of Israel out of Egypt, the Supreme Deity used Venus, the 'day star', to guide them, as he also later used it to illustrate other Jewish teachings. Thus it becomes apparent that through the course of religious history the Supreme Deity has made great use of the movements of Venus in its physical form.

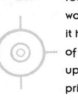

This planet is also known as the 'morning star' or the 'first star', and is a planet which litters the religious, social, and historical landscape of our world, thereby lending credence to the idea that it has powers that far surpass human wisdom. Few of us at some time in our lives have failed to look up at it in awe, and so it should come as no surprise to know that it is to this star that you should pray when you need the inspiration to break out of some difficult impasse. After all, you may not end up becoming a prophet, but with the help of the spirit worlds, and Venus in particular, you may eventually become as successful as the most astute business-man.

THE MOON

As you well know, for those of us here on Earth the heavenly body with which we are most familiar is the moon. While (in Chinese philosophy) the sun is regarded as representing the 'positive' male yang force, the moon is thought of as standing for the 'negative' female yin force.

It is also no coincidence that the pronunciation of the word for moon in Japanese, *tsuki*, sounds the same as the Japanese word for 'luck', and is used in such phrases as *tsuki ga aru* ('be lucky') or *tsuki ni mihanasareta* ('have luck pass you by').

Meanwhile, in China, when it comes to the root pictograms that together comprise Chinese written characters, the 'moon root' is used in many words concerning the body or health, including 'hips', 'liver', and 'internal organs'. Again this is no coincidence – the people living in ancient times who developed the earliest forms of Chinese characters were well aware of the moon's influence upon our health, and purposefully used the 'moon root' when devising Chinese characters for such meanings.

The atmosphere of a pale, delicate light associated with the moon perfectly corresponds to the world of Indian Buddhism, where the supreme god of the moon, Tsukiteruhiko no Ohkami, exerted immense influence over Buddhism in his capacity as guardian spirit for Gautama Buddha. Unlike the sun, the moon's light lacks the intensity to expose every nook and cranny, and is therefore a perfect reflection of a religion that appropriately recognizes the existence of carnal desire and evil passions, and yet, by subtle preaching, little by little leads the believer along the true path. Furthermore, in a country such as India, which suffers greatly from the searing intensity of the sun, it comes as little surprise that the moon has come to symbolize a cool gentleness that occupies a special place in the heart of its people.

Of course there is one other aspect of the moon that exerts a great influence over our lives, one which has been immortalized in a wealth of literature, art, and song: its power to influence the romantic course of our lives.

If you are hoping to meet the partner of your dreams you would be wise to pray to the Moon

---

You will quickly find yourself able to overcome your usual stumbling shyness or lack of confidence if you call upon the moon's powers, and instead will discover the ability of getting to know a person with the easy charm and sophistication that greatly increases your chances of finding the true love you desire.

It is interesting to see that in the astronomical scheme of things, the Earth revolves around the sun and the moon revolves around the Earth, showing that all of these celestial bodies are involved in deeply symbiotic relationships of an indissoluble nature. The sun provides power not just on a physical level, but for the spiritual world of human beings (that is the world of the soul), while the moon also heavily influences the world of the physical, as well as the divine and spirit worlds. The result for us as human beings is that, if we could just be more aware of the divine and spiritual nature of these two heavenly bodies, we would then be better able to understand the

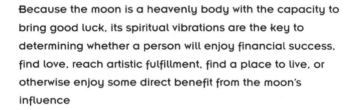

nature of their influence, and thereby be better prepared to deal with the way those influences manifest themselves in the course of our everyday lives.

Because the moon is a heavenly body with the capacity to bring good luck, its spiritual vibrations are the key to determining whether a person will enjoy financial success, find love, reach artistic fulfillment, find a place to live, or otherwise enjoy some direct benefit from the moon's influence

---

Of importance to women who are suffering from irregular periods – a condition known in Japanese as *tsuki no mono* – is the fact that prayer and pursuit of a sense of empathy with the moon will see the problem clear up completely. It is also the moon that has the capacity to heal the hearts of those who have been hurt in love. After all, when broken-hearted, it is not the sun but the moon that triggers our romantic thoughts, and gives us the tranquillity and peace of mind to place our sorrow more rationally within the greater context of our lives. Turning to the moon for relief will help a person find the courage to carry on, and the faith to believe that a truer and deeper love will appear in the future.

Of course, howling loudly at the full moon in search of solace can bring on a whole different set of problems, and is not something I, or any other decent werewolf-fearing person would recommend you to do. After all, what would your new girlfriend think if you sprouted fangs and a hairy face!

In rating the level of the spiritual world of the moon, we would have to put it in the mid- to lower-range; a place where people who have done little, whether it be for good or bad, during their life on Earth go after their deaths.

MARS

Mars is a hot, fiery planet across whose molten surface slither plagues of dark-eyed dragons; red dragons, flame dragons, and black dragons, all existing in a constant seething turmoil of conflict and simmering resentment. This planet is a world of passionate emotions and conflict; a battlefield — a killing ground where there are only two types of residents: the fast and the dead. All kinds of weapons, torture instruments and other pain-inflicting tools spawned from the most twisted of minds are stored here, on a world Nostradamus recognized in his poetic prophecies as a dark realm of death and destruction.

This unpleasant planet has a very uncomplicated atmosphere to it, which best corresponds to a child's age of two to three years old. At this age children do not know what it is to be tired, and when they see things that they want, they are likely to scream and cry until they get them in their little hands. In their new world of wonder they want to explore everything, to pick things up, throw them around, even taste them if they can — in other words, they are not satisfied simply to look at something, they always have to engage in dynamic action of some kind.

Mars is a world that is awash in spiritual vibrations of this kind. Therefore, people who lack the motivation and aggression that is sometimes a necessary requirement in life would do well to immerse themselves in the spiritual vibrations given off by this planet. The seething conflicts which permeate and bind this planet together, and which cast its influence toward the Earth, can bring powerful benefits to professional sportsmen, business people or to just about anyone who needs that spark of assertiveness required to ensure them success and long-term happiness.

JUPITER

Jupiter is the body in our Solar System that acts as a kind of facilitator for demands and requests originating from both the Earth and the Heavens. Jupiter reflects the wishes of Heaven and then influences developments here on Earth in accordance with those wishes; or alternatively, Jupiter reflects or transmits the wishes sent from Earth up to the Heavens. This function of intermediary makes Jupiter particularly effective in listening to our direct requests.

When it comes to the stage in human life that this planet best corresponds to, it would be the period lasting from the age of 11 up until the age of about 17. The planet's spiritual atmosphere, just like young adults, is imbued with the exuberant vitality and indestructible strength of adolescence, and is further characterized by a wonderful burgeoning of good fortune. This is a world that is also constantly concerned with the progress of human life, and is as a consequence full of spiritual waves replete with the spirit of beneficial change. In visual terms, its domains extend through day and night scenes of exquisite beauty, littered with structures that, in the scope of their extravagant elegance have only the romanticized spires of Disneyland as an entirely inadequate earthly comparison.

I forgot to note earlier that while Venus corresponds to the Taizo or 'Womb World' of Buddhist philosophy, Jupiter closely parallels Buddhism's Kongo or 'Diamond (Vajra) World'. Naturally, both Venus and Jupiter are quite high-level divine and spirit worlds, occupying places in the upper level of the middle-spirit worlds. This is the world where people who lead a life of positive attitude, punctuated by numerous good deeds can look forward to going when their life on Earth is over. In this spiritual world of breathtaking beauty, residents have the freedom to enjoy whatever lifestyle they choose amidst a paradise of peaceful tranquility and gentle comfort.

Praying to Jupiter is appropriate not only when you are requesting something specific, but also when you seek the influence of its spiritual vibrations — for they have the power to reinvigorate you with the lively feelings and enthusiasm of your youth. Furthermore, I would encourage teenage readers who are presently enjoying the full flush of youth to pray to Jupiter when facing periods of personal pain, sadness or failure, because this is the period of your life when Jupiter has the greatest influence.

Jupiter has a unique 'Wish Fulfillment Shrine' that listens to all petitions made to it. If you can make a special pilgrimage to Ise, Izumo, or any of the other major shrines scattered around Japan, the gods honored in those places will be suitably impressed that you have traveled so far to make your request, and will feel obligated to grant you extraordinary favors. And, by extension, if your *kushimitama* soul makes the odyssey all the way from Earth to visit the Jupiter spirit world directly and worship at the 'Wish Fulfillment Shrine', the gods of Jupiter will feel inclined to grant whatever requests you might have. (Unfortunately, up until now probably less than a few hundred people have actually done this – these of course are the people who visited Jupiter on one of my star tours.)

Within this one unique compound are actually three separate 'Wish Fulfillment Shrines': 'Rakuhokyu' (Palace of Happiness and Plenty), 'Shinsenkyu' (Palace of the Mountain Wizards), and 'Ogonkyu' (Gold Palace), which has the wonderfully elegant 'Golden Princess' as its permanent resident.

It is said that if the Golden Princess should ever smile on you, then you will be free of any kind of money worries for the rest of your life

---

Jupiter is by far and away the largest planet in the Solar System, with a gravity of such colossal magnitude that just a small increase in its specific mass would enable it to shine of its own accord, essentially taking on the appearance of a second sun within our Solar System. That being so, it appears to be a planet which contains within it immense hopes – just as a young adult harbors great unbridled promise, ready to burst into mature fulfillment. It is apparent in both cases that, hidden away from immediate view, is a great wealth of possibilities just waiting to be revealed by the person with the desire and faith to unlock the door.

SATURN

This planet is home to Enma (Yama), the King of the Dead, whom I have surprisingly got to know quite well during the several occasions I have visited the planet.

He plays demonic host to people who, while on Earth, committed murder or performed other similarly terrible deeds, by which despicable merits they now find themselves banished to this evil and forbidding hell.

There is an expression in Japanese, *shichinan hakku* ('seven difficulties and eight pains'), which in essence means an endless myriad of troubles, and which aptly describes the situation on this planet. It is a place which overflows with bitter, corrupt and malignant spiritual vibrations. Yet its overwhelming sense of impurity does not mean that there are not valid reasons why you should direct your prayers toward this planet. For example, if you want to make sure that your children have the strength not to be defeated by life's trials and tribulations, but instead wish to see them grow up to become gutsy, independent people, it is best to direct your attention to this planet. The gods will then ensure that they grow up independent and strong, blessed with the virtues of patience and forbearance.

Although existence here is quite divorced from the worlds of dreams and hopes, it is still infused with a very strong power of righteousness.

If you want to acquire the ability to differentiate good from evil, to discern wrong from right, praying to Saturn will prove useful

Unfortunately, I have not yet taken anyone on a star tour to Saturn, as there is a very real danger that one of my charges might mistakenly end up being left behind in one of the hell-worlds. It is for this reason that the gods will not authorize visits to Uranus and Neptune either, and why there are no sections on those planets featured in this book.

PLUTO

Because of the unique way in which the track of its orbit crosses with that of Neptune, at times Pluto is the outermost planet in the Solar System, while at other times it is second farthest from the sun. However, from the perspective of the divine and spirit worlds, it remains consistently the farthest planet from the sun. In the human life cycle we have referred to throughout this examination of the planets, it corresponds to the ages after 60; this is when a person comes heavily under the influence of this planet.

Whereas the sun is a place of continuous birth and creation, Pluto is a place where older, more established matters are carefully preserved or rediscovered. Life here is carried on at a more gentle pace, where the soul is at peace, and the atmosphere is rich with a contained and lazy sense of contentment. This is the world of watercolor paintings and tranquil beauty, where time passes very, very slowly. Therefore, if you want to make the twilight of your life both a valuable and productive period, it would be to your advantage to pray to the divine and spirit worlds of

Pluto. Moreover, since this is the planet dedicated to preparation of the spirit and the search for lasting truth, those people who wish to totally immerse themselves in classical studies should look to Pluto for assistance – as should students and followers of Islam (I have seen camels and Arabs living here, for this planet parallels the spiritual world of Allah and his disciples).

I would also point out that it is sometimes said that after a person marks his or her 60th birthday, there is a partial return to the psychology and attitude of childhood. In line with this cyclical way of thinking, aspects of Pluto appear as magical worlds transported from the fairytales and imaginations of our childhood – there are towering forests like those in the tale of *Snow White and the Seven Dwarfs*, peopled by elfin creatures unlike anything on Earth.

Fitting for a planet that is at the farthest extremity of the Solar System, it is a place where judgments are handed down on the merits of a person's way of life, their attitude, and the degree of satisfaction enjoyed during their life on Earth. These are not the same as those passed down by Saturn's King Enma, which are according to the strict criteria of good and evil; rather they are assessments that serve to shed a more comprehensive light upon a person's inner feelings, motivations, and sense of conscience.

A supplementary function of this planet is to provide individuals who do a great deal of spiritual study here on Pluto, with the right to journey on beyond the Solar System to the far reaches of the North Star.

THE NORTH STAR

The Earth's axis points directly towards the North Star, located within the constellation known commonly as the Great Bear. And an eternity before man became aware of the stars above his

head, or even first appeared on the surface of the planet, this alignment was already in place in a relationship that has long exerted a major influence upon our planet. When considering the most appropriate destination to address your spiritual entreaties, you should bear in mind that requests which have relevance for an entire lifetime should be addressed to the North Star; those for daily life to the sun; and special requests should be addressed to Jupiter. Couples should also try to direct requests related to the futures of their new-born children to the North Star, due to the fact that its supreme deity has a

grandfatherly quality and who therefore responds very favorably to the needs of children.

This star represents the zenith of the spiritual worlds; a heavenly home to the universal wisdom of truth in a world awash in supremely strong spiritual vibrations.

> If an individual can achieve a spiritual rapport with the celestial vibrations given off by the North Star, then they have at their fingertips the potential to harness a divine power of extraordinary magnitude

With the power of this star within your control you stand to reap a host of benefits: clarity of thinking, coolness of decision-making, professional and social success, greatly increased artistic sensibility, and the ability to avert unfortunate incidents before they can occur – all this can be yours by taking advantage of the power of the North Star.

Since the North Star is always easy to locate in the sky, it is also easy to pray to on a regular basis. It is where the Supreme God of the Universe, known to the ancient Chinese people variously as Tiandi, Taiotsu, Taikyoku, Ten no Sufu and Kyokushin (which are all actually references to the North Star) has his real residence. Within the North Star's Seigenkyu Palace live 'Taiotsu the Aged One', alongside the 'Holy Mother', and it is here that the complicated scenarios for the various dramas of human society are worked out.

The Benefits From the Stars – a Summary

THE NORTH STAR

All the huge wealth of universal wisdom and good fortune are

 embodied within the North Star. It exercises control over human development at an early stage; it can decide the initial establishment of the fetus and even the nature of its inherited traits, thereby to a large degree determining a person's entire fate. When the possibility of disaster or unfortunate events are as yet still formless, it has the ability to stop the numerous component factors coming together and allowing the disaster to become a reality. It is in this way that the star's extensive powers

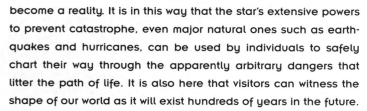

to prevent catastrophe, even major natural ones such as earthquakes and hurricanes, can be used by individuals to safely chart their way through the apparently arbitrary dangers that litter the path of life. It is also here that visitors can witness the shape of our world as it will exist hundreds of years in the future.

THE SUN

Functions as a form of central government for the Solar System. It governs activity, fame, glory, success in life, and vitality.

MERCURY

Gives off undercurrents of influence equivalent to the life period of a person between three and five years of age. A planet dedicated to acquiring knowledge, wisdom, and to search for truth. The inspiration behind both sound financial planning and melancholic songs.

VENUS

The medium for transmission of divine world wishes to be reflected on Earth. The planet of religion and spiritual studies, from which both Moses and Buddha sought direction. Corresponds to the spiritual vibrations of a person 18 to 25 years of age.

THE MOON

A manifestation of a Buddhist world that recreates the Womb World of Venus, and the Diamond World of Jupiter. Governs health and the bestowal of good luck, encompassing the possibility of financial gain and good luck in love.

MARS

The planet of endless warfare. But also overflowing with resilience and constructive energy, matching the spiritual vibrations of a person between two and three years old.

JUPITER

The planet that reflects wishes from Earth. The planet of

unlimited potential and home to the Golden Princess. Its spiritual vibrations are equivalent to those people aged between 11 and 17.

SATURN

Location of hell-worlds and a planet that is obsessed with the complex distinction between good and evil. Can provide patience and perseverance. For some reason, the planet appears to also provide relief for kidney diseases.

PLUTO

A tranquil, fairytale world. The source for traditional romanticism. Spiritual vibrations match those of people over 60 years of age. This planet can also become a person's gateway to the North Star.

THE OTHER PLANETS

Neptune has spiritual vibrations equivalent to those of a person

around six to nine years of age. Here is the hell-world to which false religious practitioners, charlatans, and diviners are ultimately condemned.

Uranus remains a world off-limits because of its function as a depository of closely guarded secrets of State administration. It controls the patterns of psychological behavior for human beings, while its spiritual vibrations correspond to those of a person between 9 and 12 years of age. Here, ego, enlightenment, and self-realization make it possible for us to understand the patterns of life. It is also the planet of reform and renewal.

ENHANCE THE LEVEL OF YOUR SOUL AND BECOME ONE WITH THE GODS

Find *Mu* in Your Heart and Draw Closer to the Gods

I am often asked by people how they can get on friendly terms with the gods. The answer is very simple. You must seek to find *mu* or 'nothingness' in your heart, and to expel all egotistical thoughts and feelings. If you can achieve this state, where you are no longer concerned with personal pride, selfishness or vanity, then, as long as you firmly believe that the gods are present within your soul, you can be assured that, as you make your way through life, the gods will be at your shoulder, gently guiding you along the way.

Develop a frame of mind in which you place everything in the hands of the gods

---

In living your own life, you must consciously try to become the kind of person that will find favor in the eyes of the gods by your inner conviction to be of service to mankind and the planet on which we live. It is important that you maintain this discipline of attitude and behavior for at least a year (or even longer), after which, in a natural fashion and when the need arises, your 'spiritual eyes' will gently open and you will be able to hear the voices of the gods deep within the recesses of your consciousness. This process of divine awakening is remarkable in its simplicity – and profound in its truth.

Of course, the history of mankind teaches us that the achievement of an ego-less state, and particularly the maintenance of it, can be an exceptionally difficult task. Accordingly, if you think that it is going to be impossible to commit to this attitude for a whole year, it is recommended that you take a step-by-step approach. At first do it for just one week, and if it works out, then continue it for the next week, until time passes and the rewards of your persistence become apparent.

In some cases, an individual may be able to hear the voices of the gods after only three weeks, while in other cases only after persevering for a full year will that eventually happen. If you treat the issue of hearing the voices of the gods as a kind of challenge, and start out by, for example, vowing to yourself,

> 'I'm going to keep going for a month. Please make sure that during that time I hear your voices,'

thereby setting some kind of deadline, it will be easier for the gods to make some kind of decisive move.

Incidentally, although here I am referring to the 'voices of the gods', in most cases what you will actually hear are the voices of your guardian spirits, who are the spiritual entities best positioned to act in an unconcerned, relaxed fashion. This is because before a person can actually hear the voices of the gods, the proper groundwork has to be laid and the proper procedures followed.

To give an analogy, it is extremely difficult to talk directly to the head of state, be it a Prime Minister, President, or whatever. It is much easier to talk to the mayor of the city or town in which you live. Nevertheless, in such a situation it would be foolish not to treat your mayor with the appropriate respect, for the mayor will no doubt have direct lines of communication to the head of state. Similarly, even though what you may really be listening to are the voices of your guardian spirits, they will still be communicating to you the true intentions of the more illustrious gods. However, in receiving these messages you must remain careful to ensure the validity of the voices you hear, because in many cases their source may be evil spirits who are purposefully trying to mislead you. This process of validation is referred to as *saniwa* or 'detecting the gods', which, although insufficient space prevents me from describing in fuller detail the methods used, relies on perception of the spiritual presence and tone of the message – or alternatively, in written messages, the spirit inherent in the style of handwriting used.

Active and Passive Spiritual Training

There are other methods for contacting the gods.

As I am sure many of you with a passing knowledge of theology will know, one method is by engaging in ascetic practices: subjecting your body to harsh environmental conditions and denial – bathing under icy waterfalls, seeking isolation from others, or fasting, for example – which perform the function of cleansing the body and soul of any evil presence, and allow the spirit of the gods to then enter the body. However, a disadvantage of this approach is that by overdoing such rigorous practices, you run the risk of weakening the body as well as the spirit, which in turn can leave you vulnerable to attack from evil spirits.

Furthermore, a person will generally not even consider undergoing such harsh spiritual training unless his desire to seek direct contact with the gods is exceptional, or there are some other special conditions involved that inspire such fanatical devotion. In such cases this extremely focused sense of resolve can gradually distort into transcendental desires, which, if they continue for some time, can then lead to dangerous spiritual imbalances. And in response to these weakening imbalances, *tengu* fox or *tanuki* racoon dog spirits, and other evil or mischievous spirits may attempt to take possession of you.

That being so, I cannot give a thorough endorsement to the ascetic approach. If you do decide to pursue this path, I would strongly urge you to train under a reputable and responsible teacher; and while continuing to live a normal lifestyle, engage in balanced training of your soul, the acquisition of knowledge, and spiritual self-realization.

Involvement in rigorous training in order to approach the gods under your own initiative is referred to in Japanese as *koten no shugyo*. As I previously explained, a simpler and far easier technique is to totally entrust your soul to the gods, and let the gods approach you – this in turn is known as *senten no shugyo*. This is a far more accessible technique that allows anyone to get in touch with the gods, and was used in the past by such significant religious figures as Christianity's Joan of Arc; Miki

Nakayama, the founder of Japan's Tenrikyo religion; and Nao Deguchi of the Omotokyo religious movement.

Let me add here that there is one other known method of contacting the gods, whereby you take advantage of a medium in order to exchange messages with the spirit world. Unfortunately, however, there is a great disparity in the spiritual power of these 'spiritualists' or 'mediums', and the degree of their spiritual training determines the extent to which they will be able to communicate with the spirits. This may well mean they are only able to communicate with spirits up to a certain level, which might not only limit their effectiveness, but may encourage them to contact spirits which have only recently died. As I explained earlier in the book, such practice is strongly disapproved of by the spirit world, and it is for this reason that I feel unable to endorse such a technique.

Four 'Souls' Determine Your Actions

Here I would like to give a more detailed explanation of the human soul or, more accurately as you will find out, 'souls'.

Just as the human body has a head, a torso, arms, and legs, so too does the human spirit have various 'souls' or *mitama* that play their own unique role. They are:

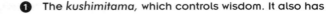 **1** The *kushimitama,* which controls wisdom. It also has

overall control over the other three *mitama,* and handles the faculties of intuition and spiritual insight.

2. The *nigimitama,* which is responsible for feelings of friendship and peace, and performs a harmonizing function. In terms of the physical body, it is responsible for the internal organs.

3. The *aramitama,* which governs courage. It corresponds to the muscles, bones, and other such components of the body. It can also express itself in terms of perseverance and resilience.

4. The *sachimitama,* which controls feelings of love. It corresponds to our emotions and the heart.

Even though each of these souls exist independently, that does not mean to say that they pull a person in all kinds of different directions – just as the eyes, mouth, nose, and ears make up the face, the four *mitama* together form a single, unified spirit. But when this unified spirit engages in activity, each component begins to display its own individuality – with the result that if one of the four *mitama* is over-emphasized, it will show up disproportionately in that person's personal characteristics.

Amongst these four, the one with the most influence is the *kushimitama,* which enters and exits the body through a point on the forehead. It is in reality only about the size of a person's little finger – although in every other respect, including the

☀

215

existence of facial features and the ability to express personality, it takes on a physical form identical to that of the person in whom it resides.

This *kushimitama* has the freedom to enter or exit its home body at any time, easily transporting between the spirit worlds, stars, and the planets in what is commonly known as clairvoyance or, more accurately, 'Heavenly telepathy'. And while the *kushimitama* is engaged in this kind of inter-dimensional travel, the host person as a consequence begins to discover the powers of prophecy: gradually perceiving that the ability to see events of the past and future, and to evaluate the spiritual worth of others, is becoming a facility within their grasp.

But no matter how much a person may want to take advantage of these powers, it continues to be something not all that easy to

do. Even someone who has devoted their whole lives to *koten* spiritual training will, in most cases, still be unable to achieve their goal. However, this is not necessarily the case with *senten* training, which involves special permission from the gods themselves for direct contact to take place – thereby liberating a person's powers of clairvoyance through the opening of their 'Heavenly eyes'. After death, it is inevitable that our *kushimitama* will separate from our material bodies and make its journey to the spirit worlds. But it remains extremely important for us to have the brief opportunity of seeing what the spirit worlds hold for us before our bodies grow old.

> The opening of our 'Heavenly eyes' enables us to understand the true aspects of the divine and spirit worlds, better preparing us to live truer lives that transcend life and death

This greater awareness of the spiritual vibrations given off by the stars and the other celestial bodies, as well as an awareness of the occasional negative influence of evil spirits, can bring with it great improvements in both your personal and professional relationships, and the amount of good fortune you come to enjoy.

Once a person manages to harness the phenomenal power of the spirit world, they will discover that ambitions that would previously have taken several years to achieve end up taking a mere fraction of that time – releasing you to pursue other projects, or to seek further understanding of the spirit world. This process creates a rewarding upward spiral.

> Increased spiritual awareness creates greater earthly ability, the success of which creates more free time to achieve more spiritual awareness, which in turn creates yet more earthly ability

During star tours, the *kushimitama* visits the various celestial bodies, directly experiencing the different spiritual aspects of each. It then transfers the experience to its host, by setting into motion subconscious processes in the brain, and then communicating the experiences through clearly defined inspiration.

However, if activity in the left side of the brain, which is responsible for deep conceptualization and calculation functions, becomes too heavy, this runs the risk that the concepts arising there will also become too dominant. This in turn will create interference with communication by the *kushimitama*, causing the clarity of its message to become affected. If, on the other hand, the person can remain calm and composed, with an attitude that says, 'I will just leave everything up to the gods,' *kushimitama* communication will occur in a very clean and precise fashion.

Unshakeable Resolution Will Bring You Good Luck

People who have achieved great success due largely to the force of their determination tend to have a certain aura to them – a sense that they are fully in touch with both themselves and with others.

If we then look for the source of this magnetism using clairvoyant techniques, we discover that in nearly all cases their respective guardian spirits and guardian gods have been heavily involved in providing the spiritual inspiration to help them in their pursuit of success.

Conversely, people who think only of themselves, who don't care about the welfare of others, tend to have practically no personal appeal – something which clairvoyant methods reveal is a consequence of our sixth sense warning us away from people who are surrounded with the presence of malign and evil spirits.

In this way we can see how the nature of a spirit that is attracted to an individual will vary greatly depending upon the strength and worthiness of that person's resolve.

The more altruistic the person's sense of determination is, the more he will succeed, and the more help he will gain from the guardian spirits and deities who recognize such positive qualities

---

Furthermore, since a person of high moral purpose is generally happy to recognize the limits of his abilities, and can detect the will of his guardian spirits in various guises, he usually doesn't suffer from an inflated ego – leaving it easy for the spirits to come to his assistance in a natural fashion, unhindered by the obstacles presented by stubborn and self-centered attitudes.

However, resolve will not be transformed into success solely on the basis of the strength of spiritual power – effort on the part of the individual himself is also required, and he must live a life in accordance with the altruistic law of the divine and spirit worlds.

The keys to success are the power of the divine and spirit worlds, together with a determined combination of your own capabilities and effort

---

Examination of the kind of spiritual support that a successful person enjoys shows us that typically he will be supported by dozens of guardian spirits, but at the same time will be doing everything within his own power to help achieve the success he desires. It is therefore fair to say that in nearly all cases the individual and his guardian spirits need to work in tandem to achieve the success the individual desires, and of which the guardian spirits approve.

If a person has a strong moral purpose, you will usually find that they walk quickly and with long strides. That is because

walking next to him and matching his purposeful strides are his powerful guardian spirit partners. So when we take the time to contemplate the direction our lives are taking, we come to realize how wonderful the feeling would be to have the true sense of purpose that comes as we walk through life with the unfailing strength of our guardian spirits at our shoulder. Such a feeling is something which lies within the grasp of all of us – all we need is the determined efforts that spring from the courage of our convictions, and a purpose worthy of our guardian spirits' support.

Strong Resolution is Your Best Weapon

Let me describe an incident that I was involved in some time ago.

A female flight attendant who had just turned 30 visited me for a spiritual consultation, where it was her intention to discuss her future marriage prospects.

I therefore made inquiries of her guardian spirits, and within the deepest layers of her own subconscious, before finally discovering that in about six months time she was destined to meet the man of her dreams. When I told her this she was delighted, and even went so far as to begin excitedly looking for a place to hold the ceremony and drawing up an extensive guest list.

The reply from the guardian spirits was genuine, but the woman let it go to her head to such an extent that, although her destined lover hadn't even appeared on the scene yet, she was already determined to marry him and had begun to think about little else but her life after marriage. These thoughts about married life, about children, and a shared apartment, became so overwhelming that she soon began to behave as if she was already actually engaged, announcing to her friends when they met, 'By the way, did you know I'm getting married soon?'

To this her delighted friends would reply, 'Really! Who's the lucky guy?'

In turn she would say in a matter-of-fact way, 'Oh, I'm going to meet him in about six months time,' a reply which understandably caused some considerable consternation among her friends.

Anyhow, that is how things turned out.

Six months passed, and the flight attendant continued to remain convinced of what the future held in store for her. Then, one day an incident occurred that left those around her gasping in astonishment. A single man who worked for the same company, whom all of her female colleagues had always thought very attractive, suddenly asked her, out of the blue, to go on a date. She happily said yes, and every-one was later amazed to learn that on that very same day the couple agreed to get married.

I must admit to being a bit surprised by this development myself, but when I later saw her, she had a look on her face that said things had turned out just as she had expected them to. It seems that the power generated by her remarkably forceful conviction actually helped cause the fates to develop in such a way as to bring about the guardian spirits' prediction.

Now let me introduce another similar incident I was involved in, again featuring a woman in her early thirties who came to visit me. She too wanted to know if she would someday meet 'Mr. Right'.

When I asked her guardian spirits about her prospects, I was told, 'A wonderful man will come into her life within the next 12 months.'

Up until this point the situation had been developing much like the previous story, but it was soon to change thereafter.

Although this woman felt that the prediction I had given her might well come true, she did not have the strength of conviction to take any active steps to prepare for it – such as considering wedding arrangements or looking for a new place to live – and instead waited with only half a belief that she would soon meet the love of her life. Seeing as how she was already 34 (which in Japan is generally considered well past the age at which most women normally marry), that wait-and-see attitude was probably understandable. It is also true that she suddenly got a flood of invitations to meetings with prospective marriage partners in arranged marriages, and that in several less formal instances a number of highly eligible men appeared in her life. Be that as it may, things never really progressed much further and, before she knew it, the one-year period mentioned in the promise from her guardian spirits had passed.

Later when I discussed the situation with her, I learned that although she had wanted to believe in the prediction, that alone was not enough for her to take the steps the flight attendant had in developing a conceptual world of her own which had her marriage at its center.

It was from these 'case studies' that I concluded that ultimate success probably depends largely upon whether the person in question can create a conceptual world centered around their intention, which then translates into an attitude and behavior which is more likely to encourage the desire to reach fruition.

It should be borne in mind that the spirit worlds are not something distant and out of reach, divorced from our own reality — rather they occupy a parallel dimension which exists alongside our own and from which we can seek both guidance and cooperation.

The spirit worlds respond in proportion to the strength of conviction of the person's desire

Say that a woman thoroughly convinces herself: 'I can get married. I and my husband will then build our future together in the following way ...' then the spirit worlds are certain to take action to make these dreams come true. Moreover, if she completely trusts in the promises of her guardian spirits and builds a world which conceptualizes the fulfillment of these wishes within her mind, there is no reason whatsoever to assume that the spirit worlds will fail to act on her behalf.

In the case of the woman who did not get married, it is likely that her guardian spirits did lay all the groundwork needed for her to pursue her dream. But unfortunately, there can also be no doubt that her attitude was not a fully committed one, and that she failed to construct a conceptual world or a spiritual foundation of belief.

From these two examples, I think we can see that the most important point when it comes to making use of the power of the spirit worlds is whether or not the individual is capable of building a conceptual world of faith around their desire, with its foundations sunk in a feeling of deep conviction.

The thoughts, desires, and concepts of which I am writing come in many forms. But the best are those motivated without concern for ego, and which by their simplicity and worthiness make it easy for the divine and spirit worlds to react favorably.

The worst possible thing you can do, as has

been stated several times previously, is to encourage thoughts of revenge, which can give birth to an *ikiryo* – a living wraith.

By developing a deep hatred for someone with constant negative thoughts of, 'I wish he were dead' or 'I hope everything goes really badly for him' – while at the same time picturing in your mind all the nasty things you would like to see happen to him – you create a rich environment for the integration of all these negative sentiments into a single living spirit that will take possession of the object of your hatred. I have had the opportunity to see spirits on many occasions, and can assure you that there is no other spirit that is as vehement and unyielding as a living wraith. Vengeance takes on this terrifying spiritual form; wrapping itself around your enemy's body in the sickly stench of its loathsome embrace, entwining its suffocating arms and legs around neck, hands, and hips, while its teeth sink deeply into flesh. Moreover, since the victims remain alive, these evil spirits can be created over and over and over again. Never tiring or giving up, they can continue to plague the person until they are drained of all resistance, leaving behind only what in spiritual terms would be considered a shriveled and dry shell.

However, at the same time, the person who has given birth to such vicious wraiths will also find himself falling into a spiritually desolate and lonely state, to be accompanied by a steadily downward spiral in the nature of his own fortunes.

Incidentally, strong thoughts, whether negatively or positively motivated, have the necessary power to influence the spirit worlds and push them into action. So if you bear this fact in mind before proceeding in life with a positive attitude – while at the same time steadily creating a conceptual world around your desires – the power of your *arayashiki* ('consciousness'), centered around your guardian spirits, will manifest itself in tremendous spiritual power that has the required strength to greatly influence the spirit worlds. By understanding and following this process, a person learns one of the key secrets to enjoying a happy and successful future.

METHODS FOR OVERCOMING EVIL SPIRITS AND THE GOD OF POVERTY

Exorcism is the Most Reliable Method

Now I would like to address the need to eliminate the negative factors that have a tendency to cast a dark pall over an individual's fortunes. By negative factors, I refer to the mean-spirited thoughts and intentions we all have from time to time, and to the evil spirits which often accompany them.

Although we speak of 'evil spirits', there are actually many different kinds. There are *kenzoku*, powerful messengers from the divine and spirit worlds; dragon deities and *inari* foxes that can actually also provide a wide range of benefits; there are spirits tied to a particular location, wandering spirits, and the other spirits of dead people; and of course there are the *ikiryo* or living wraiths.

Spirits that place obstacles in the path of an individual's pursuit of success are in most cases formed as a result of a 'cluster of resentments' – which have collected and festered sufficiently long enough for them to combine and take on a defined spiritual existence. It would be almost acceptable to us if these spirits simply exacted their revenge and then returned to the spirit world, but in more situations than might be expected this is not the case, and the resulting spiritual impediments can cause severe complications. The revengeful and malicious feelings of these spirits can be very difficult to remove, and may continue to plague the individuals concerned for years or even sometimes decades to come.

These voracious spirits have the capacity to hungrily devour any good fortune a person may have been endowed with; no matter how much the person may strive to improve his fortunes, it will generally be without success

---

One way to deal with this problem is to undergo one of the 'World Mate exorcism' rites that I occasionally supervise, the purpose of which is to untangle the evil spirits from the person they are afflicting, and to then send them back to a peaceful existence in the spirit worlds. I have conducted thousands of these exorcisms, with all but a handful being complete successes. But even with the successful performance of such rites, unless the person in question is willing to change their negative attitudes, the spirits which have been removed will all too quickly have their places taken by new and equally malevolent spiritual substitutes.

Unfortunately, as I tend to perform these exorcisms only in Japan, this will be quite impossible for many people to take advantage of. However, if there is a trustworthy spiritualist (or parapsychologist) living near you, it is probably fine to ask him or her to conduct the exorcism instead. If even this is not easily done, then you will have to rely on your faith and resolution being strong enough, by itself, to marshal the protective forces of your guardian spirits to help you overcome any negative spiritual interference.

What is certainly the most dangerous course to take is to request an unprofessional or untrustworthy spiritualist to perform the exorcism for you. Avoid such an approach at all costs, as a bungled exorcism can result in both the person conducting the exorcism, and the person undergoing it, to generate extremely strong spiritual impediments – while the spirits that the exorcism is aimed at displacing will remain firmly in place.

Avoid Impure Places

In our world, there are some places that, regardless of the influence of rational thought, still manage to fill us with feelings of dread.

Graveyards, for example, are places that are likely to give us the creeps – particularly if we are walking through them alone at night. The reason for what we see as this irrational fear is, in fact, a subconscious awareness, operating at a spiritual level, that recognizes such places as being filled with spirits of the dead.

Places that have similar characteristics, although they appear less obvious, are areas where drunks tend to hang out, red-light areas, and notorious trouble spots – all of which are places likely to be heavily influenced by the hordes of evil spirits that congregate there. And if you find yourself frequenting these kind of places with unhealthy thoughts in mind, you run the very real risk of attracting the attention of these malicious spirits.

You should also avoid houses where someone has been murdered or died an unnatural death. Although the morbid curiosity to which we are all prone may tempt you toward such places, there is a danger that the spirits of homicidal demons, pestilential deities, and other spirits that lurk around such locations will attach themselves to your presence.

Furthermore, there is even the danger that during a foreign trip you might unknowingly acquire a spiritual infestation that you unwittingly bring back home with you. The Customs agents do not check for spiritual contamination, so it is up to you alone to protect yourself from this kind of threat.

Many traditional tourist spots we tend to visit on holiday are of a religious nature; churches, temples, and pyramids are typical places whose very reason for existence is based in religious practice. However, many of these places have a history of being 'sacred land' or burial grounds, and on occasion — when government funds are not forthcoming or there is a general lack of motivation and respect — these sites can over the passage of time become deeply neglected and unclean. These neglected places have become overrun with evil spirits and are best avoided — as are the seedy and spirit-infested haunts of thieves, drunks, and the other undesirables in society that form an unfortunate sub-culture in most major cities.

I know of an example which illustrates well the dangers apparent in spending time in the more sordid pursuits that male tourists are sometimes notorious for. It occurred on the Indonesian island of Bali, and is the story of a man who went there on a week-long pleasure trip.

The man in question was half-responsible for the trouble, because while he was there he purchased the sexual favors of a young Balinese woman. This eventually turned out to be the source of his trouble, since after his little affair ended, he found himself suffering from excruciating pains that extended throughout his entire body. Upon returning home to Japan he immediately went to the hospital to seek help, but was worried to learn that the results of his examination were inconclusive. Nevertheless, the pain had become so unbearable, with painkillers having little or no effect, that in his frantic desperation to escape the torment he was increasingly seeing little alternative but suicide. As you can imagine, he was a sad and sorry sight indeed when, in one last attempt to escape the pain, he finally turned up at my Tokyo office.

As we carefully examined him, his dark air of despondency was soon lifted as we quickly realized the source of his condition – he had been enveloped by the green specter of a serpent, which had entwined itself around his body and was slowly crushing the life from his *mitama* souls. Once the nature of the problem had been properly diagnosed, it was a relatively simple matter to disentangle him from the ghost serpent by performing a quick but thorough exorcism. This understandably delighted the gentleman who, upon completion of the rite, found himself immediately free of any kind of pain. And, after expressing his immense gratitude to both me and my staff, he was then able to leave my office and make his way back to the station, barely able to hide the huge smile of relief that kept spreading across his face.

It was quite obvious that the ghost serpent had previously attached itself to the woman in Bali, but during the single night that they had spent together, had decided to 'change homes'. This was how it made its way back to Japan, and serves as a potent warning to the many men who go to resorts such as Bali in search of sexual adventure without considering the spiritual risks they expose themselves to.

Of course, tropical islands such as Bali offer some beautiful scenery and a wealth of historical and cultural interest — but aside from the warning above, you should also never be tempted to buy any religious artefacts you may be offered, for in the vast majority of cases such treasures are also accompanied by a host of evil influences, which may well join you on your return home.

The Proper Way to Honor Those Who Have Died Tragically

Stories have often reached me of how people who have taken on the painful task of gathering the remains of war dead from old battlefields, in order to conduct ceremonies which will allow their spirits to rest in peace, have later suffered from various ailments that have been very difficult to shake off. This is due to the fact that spiritual disorder has a strong tendency to develop during and after such occasions – a phenomenon which is caused by the people involved developing too great a sympathy with those who have already passed into the spiritual realm.

If a person tortures themselves with thoughts of,

'Oh, those poor, poor men – how they must have suffered. I wonder what was going through their minds when they died. If they were still alive today, they would be...'

then the very strength of their thoughts can serve to beckon the dead back to our material world. This would result in the spirits finding themselves in a situation where they are unable to fully commit themselves to the spirit world, and instead would seek to find a degree of comfort in attaching themselves firmly to the person responsible for bringing them to such an uncomfortable impasse.

Of course, after death a person no longer has the physical dimension to his being, and so is unable to fully return to our corporal world. Instead, what remains of critical concern for the spirit of the dead person at this time is not a passing flirtation with the physical world, but its total immersion into spiritual train-

ing within its appointed spirit world, and to use the benefits of that training to slowly raise its standing there.
Consequently, when commemorating the dead, we
should ask that they be granted the peace of mind to
enter the spirit world, and to begin their spiritual training
without delay.

It is of crucial importance that we never indicate our
desire for them to return to our world, as the consequences of countless spirits trapped in a tormented pur-

gatory between the physical and spiritual worlds would be
disastrous.

There are many instances of places which have borne witness
to the loss of an untold number of human lives. War graves, air
and sea disaster sites, and the massive destruction wrought by
hurricanes or earthquakes, are all locations pregnant with the
sentiment of lost human life. And although the pain in such
places is almost tangible, it is not recommended that you
become too overtly sympathetic – instead, if the dead are to
find lasting peace, we should opt for proper memorial ceremonies that respect the fundamental transition that the spirits
have undertaken, and which all of us are one day destined to
make.

Yet with the particular issue of war, there is a deeper concern;
a concern wrapped in issues of loyalty, bravery, and self-
sacrifice – and which deserves a slightly more searching
appraisal.

At all times, but especially in battle, the frame of mind at the moment that death arrives is extremely important. Dying thoughts of 'It's okay to die if it means my family will be fine,' or 'I'm content to die in the knowledge that I have helped my country,' are highly noble and courageous sentiments that, as a life is taken, guarantee that the spirit will be welcomed with honor into the spiritual domain.

This is because such thoughts illustrate that they are leaving this world with no regrets, nor with any lingering desire to cling to this life. Instead, they are peacefully and with finality leaving this world for the farther shore.

That being so, it follows that if, when dying in battle, a man's mind is full of desperate thoughts such as 'This can't be happening to me, I'm too young to die,' or 'Someone help me. I need to live!' then these thoughts have the potential to continue to live on in this world. Consequently, if you are involved in the aftermath of war, collecting the remains and belongings of the dead, it is not sufficient merely to conduct ceremonies that you think sufficient for consoling the dead and bringing comfort to your own anguish and grief. Rather, you should conduct ceremonies that in a careful and respectful way will bring lasting peace to these restless spirits.

With this law of the spirit world in mind, I continue to hope that only people who have a deep familiarity with spiritual matters be involved in the organization of those groups whose aim is to bring consolation to those whose lives were lost in war.

LOGO MARKS
FOR CORRECTLY
APPEALING TO
THE GODS

HOW TO USE THE MARKS

This chapter contains a total of 22 mysterious logo marks, of various shapes and sizes, which I have dubbed the 'Divine World Good Fortune Logo' power marks. Since these marks are referred to as 'power marks', it naturally implies that they are chock full of special powers.

In a modern context it would be best to refer to these marks as 'receiving equipment', which are responsive to the spiritual vibrations being sent out by the divine and spirit worlds – what in earlier days would have been thought of as ancient divine and spiritual symbols with the power to directly call forth the gods and spirits.

Radios and TVs receive electromagnetic waves, and then convert them into visual images and sounds. In a similar way, the Divine World Good Fortune Logo power marks have the ability to receive spiritual waves sent from benevolent stars and planets, and to manifest them here on Earth in specific forms of power that we human beings can experience.

The world is full of people who place great trust in the powers of symbols: the Star of David, the Christian cross, and the Crescent Moon and Star of Islam are all popular examples of symbols that encapsulate and channel the diverse elements of an individual's faith. But as is the case with these other symbols, unless the individual using the Divine World Good Fortune Logo marks completely believes in their abilities, they will not be able to manifest the full extent of their power. After all, no matter how high performance your radio or TV may be, if they are not connected to an appropriate power source, they amount to little more than expensive chunks of metal. In other words, it is faith that provides the power to enable your spiritual radio to work.

Now let me explain how easy it is to use these logo marks.

The first thing to do is to search for the mark among the collection that, by its significance of design and form, most closely matches your ambitions at this particular time. Make a photocopy of the mark and then fix it to your desk, bedroom wall, or personal notice board. It would be unwise to place it in too noisy a location, so try to choose as quiet a spot as you can find.

Then follow these simple steps:

1. Stare at the middle of the symbol for a minimum of one minute. (Those of you with an acute spiritual sensitivity will no doubt notice that the logo mark will begin to radiate a gold or light purple brilliance during this time.) Focus on it with the thought that the shape of the image is being transmitted through your retina and burning itself into the fabric of your subconsciousness.

2. Think to yourself that the objective you previously set yourself has already been achieved. After continuing to gaze at the mark for a full minute, you should have acquired a strong sense that you have been thoroughly enveloped by the power of the

mark, and that your wish has already been
attended to. At this point it is advisable to say out
loud, 'I have already done ...' and then complete
the sentence with exactly what you now feel has
already been achieved.

❸ Encourage the feeling that the mark, as a conduit
of the divine and spirit worlds, has taken on a
'living' presence within your consciousness.

When using a divine logo mark, simultaneously employ one of
the power calls introduced in Chapter 3, and then attempt to
apply all of the advice contained within this book – the combination of which should ensure that your allocation of good luck is
very substantially increased.

For example, use the Guardian Spirit Unification Mark with the
power call SENTEN NAMU FURUHOBIRU, or use the Good
Fortune Welcoming Mark with the 'Amaterasu Ohmikami' (TOKOTO
NO KAJIRI) or HARUCHI UMUCHI TSUZUCHI power calls. When
using the mark whose function, among others, is to elicit the help
of Kannon, the 'Goddess of Mercury' in finding you a partner, it is
probably best to use the call SENTEN NAMU FURUHOBIRU.

Because the scope of application of these marks is so broad,
it is wise to tailor the usage of them to suit your own unique circumstances and the demands they present. So go ahead and
use the marks to secure the benefits that the divine and spirit
worlds have to offer: bear in mind the points listed above; carry

small copies of the logo marks around with you at all times; and have confidence in the knowledge that a complete faith in their inherent powers will guarantee you the help we all sometimes need to fulfill our successful destinies.

But if you find yourself questioning the truth of these power logos, allowing the seeds of doubt to grow until they strangle your faith, then no amount of staring at the marks will make any difference – you will be wasting your time, and the powers of the spirit worlds will be denied to you.

Remember too that you cannot 'transfer' the power that you receive to another person, for only the person who has faith can take advantage of the power. Nor should you use the power for any kind of negative purpose or sell the logo marks for financial gain, as such actions would be sure to bring swift and appropriate punishment from the divine and spirit worlds.

THE ORIGIN OF THE MARKS

Be it a nation state, a company, or sports team, no matter what the type of group it will usually have a suitable mark, or logo, to represent it. This emblem embodies the power, philosophy, and resolve of that particular group, and often carries with it the same aura of strength as the team itself. It becomes apparent that the emblem and that which it represents form two sides of the same coin.

I think that if you consider everything that I have written up to this point, you will realize the truth that these logo marks have their origins in the divine and spirit worlds. This was confirmed when I paid a visit to the Andromeda divine world and was told by the gods,

'You had best think of them as being a kind of conduit or celestial portal through which spiritual vibrations from the divine and spirit worlds can be received on Earth. They are a gift of the gods, capable of enhancing the latent powers of your *mitama* souls.'

People blessed with great spiritual sensitivity are probably aware that these logos are capable of catching the spiritual waves given off by celestial bodies. They may even be able to appreciate the respective 'flavors' of each of the divine and spirit worlds from which they emanate – although up until now only those logo marks of proven effectiveness have been revealed to human beings.

Although I would like to give a more exhaustive explanation of the Divine World Good Fortune Logo marks and their amazing power, lack of space dictates that you satisfy yourself with the knowledge that their phenomenal capabilities are a spiritual truth – and that only your strength of faith can determine the extent to which they can help you successfully negotiate the complicated course of your life.

'DIVINE WORLD
GOOD FORTUNE
LOGO' POWER
MARKS

Note: nearly all these marks are actually already covered by intellectual or commercial copyright, or such protection has been applied for. All use of logo marks other than by purchasers of this book, unless otherwise authorized, is therefore strictly prohibited.

Stops Random Thoughts

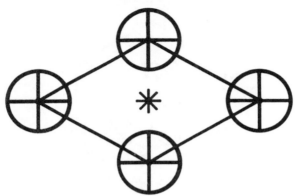

Makes the Wisdom to Discover the Truth Well Up

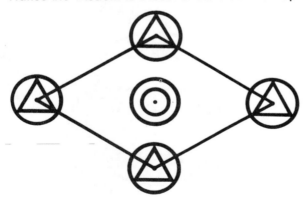

Saves Those in Hell

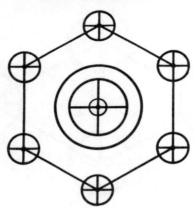

Promotes Business

Helps Find a Spouse or Lover

Increases Guardian Spirit Power for Women

サシモル ハラ チ

Improves Luck with Health

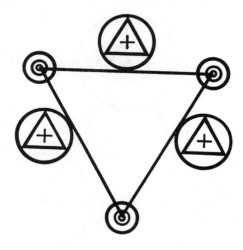

Helps to Keep You Awake

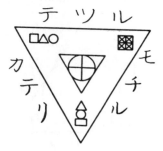

(Do not use together with the mark for inducing sleep)

Creates New Things

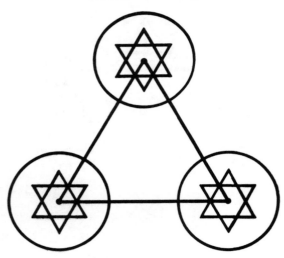

Induces Sleep

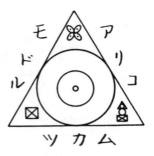

(Stare steadily at central point)

Increases Power of United Guardian Spirits

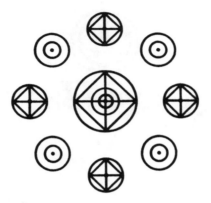

Makes It Possible to Get Along Well with Others

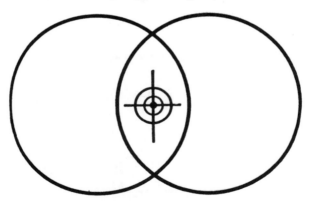

Lets You Exhibit Skills in Critical Situations

Protects Your Stomach and Bowels

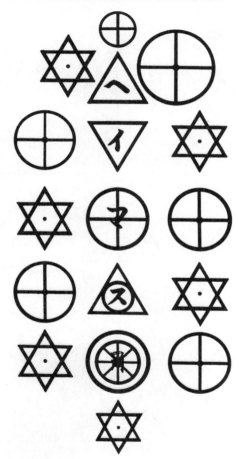

タク

ホリ

トズ

メジ

Attracts Good Fortune with Money

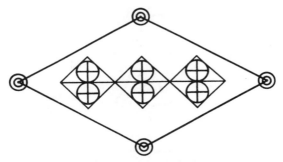

(Cross your hands and place your little fingers on the double circles to right and left)

Protects Against Disasters and Invites Happiness

Brings You Closer to Kannon (Goddess of Mercy)

(Gaze steadily at the top center diamond)

Attracts Good Fortune

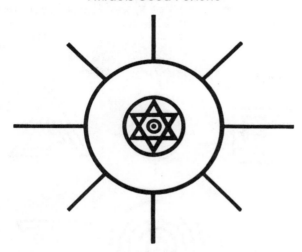

Brings People Together

Corrects Astigmatism, Near Sightedness,
Far Sightedness and Weak Vision — Makes Your Eyes
Feel Better

Concentrates Power of Gods and Spirits

WORLD MATE

World Mate is a unique organization with members of all ages and nationalities, which strives to perfect an ever-expanding climate of mutual respect that promotes the divine worlds' desire for a paradise on earth. This is sought to be accomplished by improving the level of communication among people, and between them and the divine worlds.

As a reflection of its innovative approach to the quest for lasting fulfillment in life, World Mate engages in a wide range of activities in the fields of education, social welfare, art, cultural interchange, and sport. These are very much in line with the group's basic philosophy that an individual can only achieve real happiness and self-realization if he expresses gratitude to his guardian spirits and divine benefactors, and adopts altruistic attitudes and behavior consistent with bringing happiness to others.

In addition to seminars and diverse spiritual activities, some of which are directly participated in by senior adviser Toshu Fukami, World Mate issues a newsletter and other publications for its members, and offers for sale books and tapes by Fukami, and sacred items used in ritual observances.

Branches of World Mate

UNITED KINGDOM
World Mate London
Cobham Gate
32 Anyards Road
Cobham
Surrey KT11 2LA

UNITED STATES
World Mate Arizona
5615N Acoma Drive #33
Glendale
AZ 85306

World Mate Chicago
#1602, 1660 North Lasalle Street
Chicago
IL 60614

World Mate Los Angeles
#1707 Wilshire Estina
10390 Wilshire Boulevard
Los Angeles
CA 90042

World Mate New York
Trump Palace #36B
200 East 69th Street
New York
NY 10021

World Mate San Francisco
555 Starboard Drive
San Mateo
CA 94404

AUSTRALIA
World Mate Perth
Unit 15A
Victoria Street
West Perth, WA6005